Caring for INFANTS & TODDLERS in Groups

Developmentally Appropriate Practice

SECOND EDITION

DAP-II

By
ZERO TO THREE

ZERO
TO
THREE®

National Center for Infants, Toddlers, and Families

Washington, DC

Published by

ZERO
TO
THREE®
National Center for Infants, Toddlers, and Families

ZERO TO THREE
Toll-free orders (800) 899-4301
Fax: (202) 638-0851
Web: http://www.zerotothree.org

The mission of the ZERO TO THREE Press is to publish authoritative research, practical resources, and new ideas for those who work with and care about infants, toddlers, and their families. Books are selected for publication by an independent Editorial Board.

These materials are intended for education and training to help promote a high standard of care by professionals. Use of these materials is voluntary and their use does not confer any professional credentials or qualification to take any registration, certification, board or licensure examination, and neither confers nor infers competency to perform any related professional functions.

The user of these materials is solely responsible for compliance with all local, state or federal rules, regulations or licensing require-ments. Despite efforts to ensure that these materials are consistent with acceptable practices, they are not intended to be used as a compliance guide and are not intended to supplant or to be used as a substitute for or in contravention of any applicable local, state or federal rules, regulations or licensing requirements. ZERO TO THREE expressly disclaims any liability arising from use of these materials in contravention of such rules, regulations or licensing requirements.

Cover and text design: K Art and Design, Inc.

10 9 8 7 6 5 4 3 2

ISBN 978-1-934019-26-9

Printed in the United States of America

Suggested citation: ZERO TO THREE. (2008). *Caring for infants and toddlers in groups: Developmentally appropriate practice* (2nd ed.). Washington, DC: Author.

Table of Contents

Acknowledgments

Here at ZERO TO THREE we strongly believe that early experiences matter. Research has proven that the care and resources provided for infants and toddlers by parents and other adults have an enduring effect on the children's lifelong health and development. ZERO TO THREE's multidisciplinary approach to child development brings together the perspectives of many fields and specialties and relies on robust research studies to provide information that can be used to promote each child's overall health and well-being in the context of his family and culture.

The experience of creating this new second edition of *Caring for Infants and Toddlers in Groups: Developmentally Appropriate Practice (Caring: DAP-II)* has served as an excellent example of the spirit of collaboration and community that is the cornerstone of our values and grounds the work that we do at ZERO TO THREE. *Caring: DAP-II* builds on a strong foundation laid by the original authors and layers on the latest thinking and research about quality infant–toddler care. We are grateful to the many experts and voices that helped shape this outstanding resource and are especially thankful for the knowledge and expertise brought to life in this manuscript through the writing of Sandy Petersen. In conceiving the update of this book, Emily Fenichel had the foresight to engage Betty Bardige as an early author and we deeply appreciate Betty's contributions. We also thank Libby Zimmerman and acknowledge her helpful assistance during the early stages of this work.

Many talented staff at ZERO TO THREE contributed their time and skill to shape this book into the outstanding resource guide that it now represents. We are also grateful for the expert review provided by our Board members J. Ronald Lally and Jeree Pawl and for the insight provided by Virginia Casper.

The thoughtful illustrations in the book were created by Robert Saunders, and the photographs that help to bring to life the concepts and practices detailed in this book were taken by Stephen Bobb. These illustrations and photographs were obtained thanks to the support of the Carol Berman Fund, established by Michael Berman to honor the memory of his wife and our esteemed Board member and colleague. A generous grant from the Smith Richardson Foundation allowed us to supplement *Caring: DAP-II* by providing funds for the creation of the "Behavior Has Meaning" wheel and the "Grow With Me From Birth to Three" posters that accompany this book.

Lead Writers:
Sandy Petersen
Betty Bardige

ZERO TO THREE Staff Contributors:
Emily Fenichel
Linda Gillespie
Michelle Martineau Green
Claire Lerner
Jennifer Moon Li
Sarah Merrill
Florence Nelson
Rebecca Parlakian
Amanda Perez
Victoria Prieto
Tabitha Temple
Tammy Mann

ZERO TO THREE Board Reviewers:
Ron Lally
Jeree Pawl

ZERO TO THREE Press Editorial Board Reviewer:
Virginia Casper

Introduction

What an exciting yet challenging moment in history this is for babies, families, and their teachers. It is wonderful because science has confirmed the critical importance and greatly elevated our appreciation of the first 3 years. It is challenging because of the awesome responsibility we have in caring for our youngest. What we do really matters—every little interaction, especially the little interactions—can have an impact for a lifetime.

Caring for Infants and Toddlers in Groups: Developmentally Appropriate Practice, Second Edition *(Caring: DAP–II)* describes our current understanding of early development and explores the elements of quality in group care that support strong relationships and positive learning experiences. It reflects the major concepts articulated in the National Association for the Education of Young Children position paper on developmentally appropriate practice (National Association for the Education of Young Children, 2008). It presents stories that exemplify responsive, relationship-based practice, and provides examples of reflective practice in early group care.

Understanding How Relationships Matter to Development

> "Most vital…is that the infant or toddler is cared for in ways that promote his feeling effective, respected, and understood."
>
> —Jeree Pawl (1990, p. 5)

Development in the first 3 years is a complex process, as all areas of development are interdependent—each affecting and being affected by others. New accomplishments in any one area, such as vision, enable changes in other areas, such as motor development. For example, at around 9 months a baby's vision sharpens, thus allowing her to focus on small objects. At this time, she is also able to sit independently and use her arms and hands. These developments also make it possible for her to begin to use a coordinated pincer grasp to pick up the small object she can now see.

A baby's developmental path may unfold unevenly. He may move forward, reach a plateau during which development seems to pause while the new accomplishment solidifies, then forward movement continues. Each baby's development also follows its own path at its own rate, which is based on the baby's constitutional makeup as well as her interests, skills, and experiences. One baby may walk at 9 months, another not until 15 months. One baby begins using words before her first birthday while another 1-year-old does not use words but uses sounds and actions to communicate effectively. One way or another, in these 3 short years, babies grow from the total dependency of life in the womb to being runners and jumpers, talkers who make their ideas and needs known, storytellers, artists, builders, helpers, and friends.

Photo credit: Stephen Bobb

In whatever way a child's development proceeds, it unfolds within the contexts of his relationships with the primary people within his life. These relationships are of primary importance to the child. "New evidence shows that these relationships actually shape brain circuits and lay the foundation for later developmental outcomes, from academic performance to mental health and interpersonal skills" (National Scientific Council on the Developing Child, 2004). An overall understanding of how development proceeds allows adults to offer the meaningful experiences and relationships that promote healthy overall development in these early years.

One of the major challenges to quality care for infants and toddlers in groups is sustaining responsive, ongoing, meaningful relationships between babies and their infant care teachers. These relationships need to be supported and sustained among infant care teachers and families, among the group of infant care teachers, and among teachers and their program directors. Through caring relationships in the first 3 years of life, babies and toddlers are able to do the following:

- *Develop a sense of trust in others to keep them safe and care for them.* The experiences within these first relationships provide the baby with the feeling that the world can be safe and predictable. His feelings, needs, and interests will be understood and are important to others.

- *Develop the confidence and abilities to follow their own interests as they explore and learn.* Given an interesting environment and adults who celebrate and nurture early learning, a baby will come to understand who she is and what to expect from other people as well as explore and begin to understand the world around her. She will master her home language and other languages if she is consistently exposed to them. She will learn to use her body for movement and her hands and fingers for an endless variety of tasks.

- *Build a sense of identity.* Through their experiences with exploration, and their interactions with others, each baby begins to construct an internal picture of who he or she is. From very early in life, this picture includes an understanding of how people in a baby's family and culture behave toward others.

- *Establish the basic structure of their brains.* Early experiences create physical connections in the brain, literally building the structure of the brain moment by moment.

- *May be identified as having delays or disabling conditions.* It is not always easy to tell the difference between typical variations in development and a developmental delay that needs attention. Group care is a potential setting for identifying concerns, engaging children's strengths, addressing areas of weakness, and supporting early intervention partnerships.

What Brain Research Tells Us

Research on the development of the brain has revealed the following:

- *Babies' brains grow more rapidly in size and complexity in the first 3 years than during any other period (except before birth).* Through responsive relationships and interaction with their environment, babies' brains store knowledge and develop connections that enable them to process information rapidly.

- *The brain develops sequentially.* Connections that process basic information are wired before those that process more complex information. If lower level circuits are not wired properly, higher level learning is more difficult.

- *Biology and experience interact to build the architecture of the brain.* Frequent, positive interactions with attentive adults play a critical role. Stable, caring relationships that provide security, emotional connection, and positive learning opportunities are necessary for babies' brains to develop properly.

- *All babies are born "wired for feelings and ready to learn"* (National Research Council & Institute of Medicine, 2000). The natural human desires to connect with others, explore the environment, and master skills make babies active learners who construct their understanding of the world.

- *Brief stress challenges babies to develop coping and "self-regulation" skills.* With support and practice, babies learn to control their emotions, physiological responses, and behavior. However, repeated exposure to overwhelming stress such as fear, hunger, or frustration produces toxic hormones that damage the developing brain.

Understanding How Quality Matters

> "The positive relation between child care quality and virtually every facet of children's development that has been studied is one of the most consistent findings of developmental science."
>
> —*National Research Council and Institute of Medicine (2000, p. 313)*

Developmentally appropriate programs for infants and toddlers must be structured in ways that support early relationships. Programs need to provide small group sizes, low child-to-teacher ratios, primary caregiving, a high level of teacher training, and a nesting of supportive adult relationships in order to offer meaningful, positive day-to-day experiences.

The infant–toddler care teacher needs to engage in close relationships with babies and the adults who are important in their lives, to understand development, to provide appropriate environments for babies, to create plans that meet the children's individual needs, and to understand and respond to the individual and cultural needs of each child and family. This is rewarding, challenging, and professional work.

In order for the infant–toddler care teacher to do this complex and intimate work, she must also have a system of support. This system is built on the daily interactions of personal relationships. One aspect of these relationships is the casual sharing of daily events between families and infant care teachers. Another aspect of this relationship-based system includes the teaching staff sharing pleasant, personal exchanges as well as opportunities for teaching staff to share observations and plan together.

Photo credit: Jennifer Rasmussen

Photo credit: ©iStockphoto.com/Tomasz Markowski

Structural elements of each program and the larger system of infant–toddler care support these layers of relationships. The major structural areas of quality discussed in this book are as follows:

1. Promotion of health and well-being

2. Developmentally appropriate practice

3. Program structures that support relationships

4. Family and community partnerships

5. Responsible financial and program management

Describing Quality in a Changing Landscape

The use of infant–toddler child care has grown exponentially since ZERO TO THREE published the first edition of *Caring for Infants and Toddlers in Groups* in 1995. In addition, and equally important, the demands on the workforce have increased. There are more babies in care, the population has become more culturally and ethnically diverse (bringing a variety of expectations and beliefs about care to the field), and research increasingly stresses the impact of quality on the children and families.

- According to a longitudinal study of babies born in 2001, 50% of the children were in some kind of regular nonparental child care arrangement at 9 months of age: 26% were in relative care (often with grandmothers), 15% were in nonrelative care (either in their own or in another family's home; i.e., family child care), and 9% were in center-based care.

- The population of infants and young children in group care is becoming increasingly diverse, reflecting the U.S. population in terms of race, ethnicity, and home languages. The U.S. Census Bureau estimated that non-Hispanic Whites accounted for approximately 56% of the under-5 population in 2005 (U.S. Census Bureau Population Estimates Program, 2006).

- Research continues to confirm the positive impact of high-quality group care for infants and young children, especially those living in high-risk family environments. The federal government, states, and communities have invested in a wide variety of strategies to improve the quality of infant–toddler group care in homes and in centers, to support care teachers, and to build statewide early care and education systems for children birth to 5 years or birth to 8 years.

- More babies and toddlers are entering group care of various types. Much of the increase is a result of the 1996 "welfare reform" legislation, the Personal Responsibility and Work Opportunity Reconciliation Act, which required parents to seek work or participate in training or other activities as a prerequisite for receiving public assistance. Many states exempt single parents of infants less than 1 year old, but a substantial number do not. As a result, a large number of infants and toddlers from low-income families are placed in out-of-home care.

Throughout the book, *Caring: DAP–II* addresses the varied settings in which babies are cared for in groups and explores the richness that increasing cultural diversity brings to infant–toddler care.

- Chapter 1 describes early development, the role of the infant care teacher, and the teacher–parent alliance.

- Chapter 2 explores the elements of quality for group care.

- Chapter 3 provides resources for further learning, which include tools for reflective practices, a chart of developmental milestones, and recommended references and training materials.

Caring: DAP–II is designed to help the infant–toddler care teacher and program manager recognize—and communicate to others—the knowledge and skills that are needed to provide a nurturing group care environment. By describing and exploring the experiences and dilemmas that young children, infant care teachers, and families face every day, we hope to illustrate the tremendous opportunities for development that responsive, relationship-based caregiving offers to children and adults alike.

The Revised Edition of *Caring: DAP-II*

Caring: DAP-II has been an important resource for the infant–toddler child care field since its publication in 1995. This revised edition retains the emphasis on relationships and reflective practice that has made such a contribution to the field over the past decade. This edition has some useful changes as well.

Caring: DAP-II recognizes the cultural diversity of the workforce and the families we serve and reflects the complexity and strong feelings that cultural differences may evoke. There are more descriptions of the difficulties and pressures of caring for very young children in groups as care teachers balance many urgent, conflicting needs. With acknowledgment of these pressures, there is a new emphasis on the importance of the support given by adults to other adults within infant–toddler programs. Additional information on the importance of language development and peer relationships is included with an overall updating of current research.

Two sections of *Caring: DAP-II* have changed considerably. The elements of quality have been expanded, and they include a short section on the exciting new efforts in states to build systems that support quality in early care and education. The final section, which includes tools for reflective practices, has replaced the section on appropriate and inappropriate practices with examples of good practice followed by reflections on what made these practices a better choice.

ZERO TO THREE hopes that *Caring: DAP-II* will be an important and useful resource to the infant–toddler field.

Photo credit: Stephen Bobb

References

National Association for the Education of Young Children (NAEYC). (2008, February). *NAEYC position statement on developmentally appropriate practice, 2008 Revision*. Retrieved March 13, 2008, from www.naeyc.org/about/positions/pdf/draftdap0208.pdf

National Scientific Council on the Developing Child. (2004). *Young children develop in an environment of relationships: Working Paper No. 1*. Retrieved February 18, 2008, from www.developingchild.net/pubs/wp-abstracts/wp1.html

National Research Council & Institute of Medicine. (2000). *From Neurons to Neighborhoods: The Science of Early Childhood Development* Committee on Integrating the Science of Early Childhood Development. Jack P. Shonkoff & Deborah. A. Phillips, Editors. Board on Children, Youth, and Families, Commission on Behavioral and Social Sciences and Education. Washington, DC: National Academy Press.

Pawl, J. (1990). Infants in day care: Reflections on experiences, expectations, and relationships. *Zero to Three, 10*(3), 1–6.

Shore, R. (1997). *Rethinking the brain*. New York: Families and Work Institute.

U.S. Census Bureau Population Estimates Program. (2006). National sex and age: 2000–2005. Retrieved October 14, 2007, from www.census.gov/popest/national/asrh/NC-EST2005-sa.html

Photo credit: Andrea Booher

CHAPTER 1

Development in the First 3 Years of Life

Photo credit: Stephen Bobb

Scientists all over the world are studying how very young babies listen to language; understand number concepts; learn from their changing perspectives as they roll over, sit, and stand; and always...always how they count on trusted adults to help them gain new awareness of themselves, others, and the world.

We are learning why relationships are so important to development. We are learning about individual differences such as temperament and developmental challenges, the influence of a family's and community's cultural beliefs, and the impact of early experiences on the brain. Because so many babies are in nonparental care, we are also studying both the positive effects and the challenges of providing group care for infants and toddlers.

Group care may provide unique opportunities to support relationships and learning. Infants and toddlers develop expectations about people and about themselves on the basis of how parents and others treat them. It is exceedingly important that in these first relationships, babies experience sensitive, affectionate care. When infants learn that adults meet their needs predictably and consistently, trust and emotional security develop. At the same time, infants and toddlers develop self-confidence as the adults around them help them master challenges in the world.

- Young infants (Birth to 9 months) seek *security*.

- Mobile infants (8 to 18 months) eagerly engage in *exploration*.

- Toddlers (16 to 36 months) continue to form their *identity*.

Security, exploration, and identity formation are all important developmental factors in relationships and learning throughout the first 3 years of life. However, each dominates a different period. Security is the prime motivation for the young infant. Responsive adults help young infants to feel comfortable and to be focused as they develop a sense of trust in the adult's ability to understand them, keep them safe and secure, and make predictability possible.

Mobile infants rely on this foundation of security as they feel secure to move and explore. The quality of their experience as explorers becomes incorporated into their sense of who they are. They may begin to think of themselves as "someone who can make things happen and can learn about how my world works." As they venture out, they will check back with the adult to make sure they are safe. They also count on the adult to provide rich opportunities for them to investigate the world.

Although toddlers are naturally still very involved in exploration, this period of development is dominated by the work of forming an identity. As a toddler comes to understand his own experience and becomes aware of the experiences of others being separate from his, he is solidifying his sense of self.

Throughout the first 3 years of life, each child's development needs to be understood within the context of her relationships. Sensitive parents and teachers respond to all of the ways that infants and toddlers communicate their feelings, interests, and distress. They also change their actual responses as infants and toddlers grow. Providing security for a 6-month-old who is still establishing her sense of trust in the adult is a different challenge, for example, than providing security for a 12-month-old who is consumed with the urge to explore but needs to feel secure in order to venture into new territory. Nonetheless, the need to read the child's signals and to respond to what the child needs remains the same.

This chapter on development uses the central motivation of each period as an organizing principle as we describe

Photo credit: Marilyn Nolt

the child's emerging capabilities, how infant care teachers can support development in a group setting, and how families and infant care teachers create an alliance to support the child and each other.

Young Infants (Birth to 9 Months)

Young infants need security most of all. They thrive on the warmth and caring that come from close relationships. Having someone special who responds quickly to their cues helps babies build a base of security that will support their exploration, learning, and identity formation.

The Child

Babies are individuals with individual caregiving needs. Even newborns differ from one another in their biological rhythms and the way they use their senses (sight, hearing, touch, smell, and taste) to learn about the world around them. By the time they enter child care, most babies will have established distinct sensory preferences and activity patterns.

Babies enter the world ready for relationships. Very young infants show a particular interest in the people around them. They like to look and listen; they follow the father's voice as well as the mother's. Babies recognize and show interest in the sounds of their family's language, already heard for months in the womb. They look intently at the light and dark contours of the human face, and can discriminate between an accurate drawing of a human face and one in which the main features are out of place. They can match the emotional tone of language with the expression on a person's face. Babies have many ways to participate in relationships.

By the time they are 3 months old (a time when many infants are first placed in group care settings), they are masters at attracting and holding the attention of familiar, responsive people. They can smile, laugh, cuddle, coo, reach out, and hold tight. They engage with their parents and infant care teachers in back-and-forth exchanges of gazes, grimaces, and grins. Adults learn how to understand these messages over time.

Babies delight in hearing language. They smile and gurgle when talked to and develop different types of cries to express different needs. Long before they speak in words, infants coo, babble, and then make sounds that imitate the tones and rhythms of adult talk, particularly those of their families and home culture. Before they understand even simple word combinations, they read gestures, facial expressions, and tone of voice and participate in the turn-taking of conversation. An infant just a few months old will engage as a conversational partner: she coos, her infant care teacher coos back, and the infant coos in reply. If one partner turns away or becomes distracted, the other partner calls her back with a gesture or sound. Some particularly social babies even "converse" with each other!

Toward the end of the early infancy period, babies enjoy learning simple back-and-forth games that are traditional in their culture or that of their infant care teachers. Peek-a-boo, pat-a-cake, "I roll the ball to baby," and hand-clapping games like *Debajo de un botón* are just a few of the games that many infants learn.

Babies learn through movement. As they move their arms, legs, and other body parts, and encounter the world through touching and being touched, babies become more aware of how their bodies move and feel. They soon discover that they can change what they see, hear, or feel

On Monday morning, Janeen greets Davis and his father at the door. "Hi, Davis! Hi Michael!" "Aiii! Aiii!" says Davis (6 months old), waving his arms. "Wooeee! What a hello! Look at those hands! Good to see you, little guy." Michael and Janeen talk about Davis's weekend and his morning, pausing from time to time to let Davis babble happily in response to their conversation. "Davis, you have so much to say!" says Janeen. Davis moves his arms and legs and turns his body back and forth so he can look at both Janeen and his father. "Let's go play. Where should we play?" Janeen holds her arms out, and Davis's father places a kiss on his cheek as he confidently hands Davis over to Janeen.

Illustration: Robert Saunders

As Davis's father and his teacher talk about his weekend, they look at Davis and engage his attention. He happily joins in their conversation, gesturing his greeting, turning from face to face to watch as well as listen to the language, and babbling away when they pause to give him a turn to "talk." His transition from his father to his teacher is a smooth one because both are tuned in to his needs and understand his communications. ✪

Photo credit: ©iStockphoto.com/Brandon Clark

through their own actions—how delightful to kick, see the mobile move, and be able to do it again!

Babies learn best when they are alert and calm. They can become deeply engrossed in practicing a newly discovered skill, like putting their hands together to grasp an object or batting at a mobile circling over their crib. Through the repetition of actions, they develop their large and small muscle skills and physical strength. They explore objects, people, and things by kicking, reaching, grasping, pulling, and letting go. Babies enjoy looking at family pictures and at board books with pictures of other babies.

In a group setting, young infants like to watch other babies and older children, and they light up when a friend smiles and coos at them. Many young babies enjoy being "part of the action," at least for short periods. At the same time, they can be overwhelmed by too much social stimulation, and their excitement can turn quickly to tears. They depend upon adults to respond to their signs of interest, overstimulation, fatigue, or boredom and to help them keep their excitement or distress within bounds.

Babies use their senses and emerging physical skills to learn about the people and objects around them. They touch different textures and put things in their mouths. Babies learn to anticipate how familiar adults will respond to them, a skill that will evolve much later into an ability

to "read" people and anticipate how to behave in new situations. Ideally, young infants are learning that their needs are understood and will be met. They are learning that new skills and new experiences most often bring pleasure, that determined efforts can lead to success, and that those they love will share their joy at each new accomplishment. These early experiences build a child's confidence, affecting her approach to learning far into the future.

The Infant Care Teacher

The infant care teacher's responsive interactions help infants believe the world is safe, interesting, and orderly—a place where infants are understood and their actions bring pleasure to themselves and others. Like dancers, the infant care teacher and infant synchronize their interactions, each responding to and influencing the other. The challenge is doing this with three, four, or five infants at once.

Infant care teachers need layers of supportive adult relationships themselves in order to be ready for these fleeting but highly meaningful moments of responsiveness they provide. Within a program, fellow teachers or assistants often share casual moments of friendship and helpfulness. They may help each other manage the stresses of the day and share the joyful moments. Families, by sharing information or demonstrating appreciation, may support the infant care teacher's sense of the worthiness of her work. Directors and supervisors should provide a supportive, reflective environment that offers a range of opportunities for staff to understand and manage the many feelings elicited by working with infants and toddlers. The chance to discuss the children in their care with fellow teachers and supervisors can deepen an infant care teacher's understanding of each child and of herself and can promote creative, responsive, and individualized planning.

The infant care teacher's task is to learn each baby's individual eating and sleeping rhythms, how he approaches new objects and people, and how he prefers to be held for feeding, sleeping, or comforting. While the adult learns to predict what the infant needs and how he will respond to different kinds of experiences, the baby is learning what to expect from his infant care teacher. The infant's feelings of safety, security, and confidence grow with his sense that the people and the world around him are predictable and offer interesting experiences.

The infant care teacher must be comfortable with this intimate physical care and the vulnerability and dependency of the first months. The young infant's day revolves around caregiving routines: diapering, dressing, eating, and sleeping. These routines offer important opportunities for one-to-one interaction involving talking, laughing, rocking, singing, and touching. Over time, the baby will learn to participate and even "help" during routines (e.g., by holding on to a bottle or lifting his arms or legs). The infant care teacher devotes this time to each baby while remaining aware of the other children in the room—not an easy task.

To help make this task easier, each area where routines take place should be carefully planned so that the infant care teacher's time in preparation and sanitation procedures, like getting needed supplies and careful hand washing, can be handled efficiently, leaving more time for interaction with the baby. During diapering, for example, pictures and objects at the infant's eye level capture his interest while clean, safe, and warm surfaces help him feel comfortable and secure. A mirror over the changing

table or a few easy-to-sanitize toys kept nearby can invite play and prompt further conversation while the infant care teacher attends to the baby's needs. When routines are pleasurable, infants learn that their needs and their bodies are important.

Both during and between routines, young infants need many opportunities to sample a variety of sensory and motor experiences. Before they can creep or crawl, babies depend on adults to carry them to places where there is an interesting object or activity. They need to spend some time being carried and cuddled, and some time on the floor or another firm surface where they can move freely. "Tummy time" preferably occurs near other babies with whom they can share smiles and touches. A trusted adult stays nearby to place toys within reach or just beyond, and encourage their efforts and explorations.

A well-organized environment offers babies a comfortable mix of familiar and new experiences that each infant can engage at his own pace and in his own way without becoming overwhelmed. Intriguing objects rest on low shelves or hang where they can be watched, batted, kicked, or safely tugged. However, most important to the baby is having the trusted infant care teacher close at hand.

Photo credit: Marilyn Nolt

The Infant Care Teacher/Family Alliance

For families and infants, entering child care is a transition that, among other things, means building new relationships. By the time an infant enters group care, parents have learned a great deal about their baby. The baby has also learned a great deal. She has learned to expect a certain pattern of response from her immediate family— a pattern that reflects the values, culture, and child-rearing beliefs of the family and community. For example, the family may believe that infants should never be away from an adult and that adults must respond immediately to the smallest sign of distress. The infant will expect this pattern from her primary infant care teacher in the group care setting. The infant care teacher, however, may believe that waiting a few moments helps the child to become more independent over time. It will take time for the baby to adjust to differences in adults' responses, touch, tone of voice, and the sights, sounds, and smells of a new environment.

To build solid relationships at the beginning of an infant's child care experience, infant care teachers need to observe and learn from the experiences, knowledge, culture, and child-rearing beliefs of family members. The partnership grows when infant care teachers value the family as the primary source of information about the child, and as the constant in the baby's life, and the family values the knowledge and personal characteristics of the infant care teacher. The parent–infant care teacher relationship becomes one of mutual support and learning about how best to care for the baby—an alliance is created.

Photo credit: Kelly Rozwadowski

Establishing and maintaining the alliance between parent and infant care teacher requires ongoing communication. The infant care teacher sets aside time to communicate with parents through written notes, photographs, telephone calls, casual conversation, and scheduled meetings. This way, the family and infant care teacher can share information about the baby's health, sleeping, eating, and elimination patterns, as well as her interests and accomplishments. The infant care teacher uses her observational skills to learn more about the individual baby's needs, interests, preferences, and particular ways of responding to people and things. The knowledgeable infant care teacher can anticipate new developmental challenges and help the parent adjust to the changes in behavior and moods that often accompany a baby's intense effort to master a new skill.

Families and infant care teachers may have different perspectives on what a baby needs or the best way to meet his needs. The skilled infant care teacher listens and watches for such differences, and approaches these as opportunities to learn more about the family and their community. Acknowledging and giving equal validity to different perspectives provides an opportunity to build the alliance, thus creating an environment for the baby that reflects his home experience.

Good communication skills help the infant care teacher learn from the baby's family how his behaviors and reactions reflect his individual style, physical needs, and home experience. These skills, which take time and training to develop, also help the infant care teacher discuss openly with the family any differences and hopefully arrive at a mutually satisfying solution. This form of dialogue becomes easier as the family–infant care teacher relationship grows stronger.

For parents, leaving their young infant in the care of someone else is difficult. Parents have varied reactions to this experience and express their feelings in a variety of ways. Many parents are able to negotiate this phase and form an open, caring relationship with their child's infant care teacher. Some parents are clearly sad and need more emotional support and reassurance. Others steel themselves by acting aloof; they may even appear uncaring. Others may become competitive with the infant care teacher. Becoming sensitive to differences in how parents express their feelings requires time and training.

Infants and toddlers evoke strong feelings in adults—both family members and infant care teachers. Recognizing, accepting, and working to overcome conflicting feelings are just some of the major challenges of sharing care effectively. For infant care teachers, the availability of

Catori's (7 months) pediatrician had suggested trying a strict daily eating and sleeping schedule because the baby was not gaining weight adequately and was not settling into any kind of daily schedule. Maddie, the family child care provider, adopted the pediatrician's suggested routine at the parents' request. As she got to know Catori, though, she felt that Catori needed more flexibility. Maddie told Catori's parents how she was having a difficult time getting Catori to sleep, that Catori was cranky and hungry a half hour before her scheduled feeding time, and that she got angry when Maddie tried to insist that Catori finish her bottle. Soon, though, Maddie felt she was failing Catori and was sometimes ignoring the two toddlers she also cared for. She decided to have a serious discussion with Catori's parents about the possibilities of giving up the fixed schedule.

Sitting in her living room, Maddie described to Catori's parents what she observed and asked whether either parent was seeing similar behavior at home. They said that, despite the doctor's recommendations, they also saw early signs of hunger or fatigue and that Catori seemed much happier when they responded right away. The parents were torn about disregarding the doctor's ideas, but thought Maddie's observations made sense. They liked Maddie's ideas about ways to catch Catori's early signs so that she could learn to follow her own body signals. Catori's parents agreed to discuss these concerns with the pediatrician.

After her conversation with Catori's parents, Maddie was relieved because such negotiations do not always go well. There are many reasons parents might want a particular routine: it has worked well for them so far; it is what they know from their own upbringing; it may be valued in their culture; they may have read something that suggested this approach as best for their baby; or, as in Catori's case, a health professional may have suggested the schedule. Catori's parents came from a community in which medical professionals, or other healers, were highly respected authorities.

Maddie's good communication skills, careful observation, knowledge of child development, and respectful approach helped her and Catori's family trust their own shared and developing understanding of Catori's emerging needs. By carefully observing and responding to her signals, Catori's parents stayed focused on her individual needs. Focusing on her behaviors helped both parents and teacher avoid slipping into a confrontation about who knows what is best for the child—a kind of competition the experienced provider knows is never productive. ✪

a supportive supervisor and opportunities to reflect on the emotional aspects of this work can be very helpful. Coworkers can remind each other about their unique role in developing close and caring relationships with the babies while always trying to support the infant–parent relationship. Infant care teachers can help parents, in turn, by taking every opportunity to point out to parents their baby's need and love for them. This will help parents feel comfortable leaving their baby in the child care setting while staying emotionally close, certain that they are still the most important people in their baby's life.

Young infants thrive on responsive caregiving, an engaging environment, and unhurried time to experience the simple joys of being with others. Knowledge of early development and skill in observation help both parents and infant care teachers be more responsive to babies, whose needs, moods, and interests can vary from moment to moment. The alliance between parent and infant care teacher has many benefits for the adults; but, most important, it helps them provide better and more responsive care for the baby.

Mobile Infants (8 to 18 Months)

As infants become mobile, exploration takes center stage. Like little scientists, they investigate everything they can get their hands—or mouths—on. "What will happen," they seem to ask repeatedly, "if I push this button or pull on this blanket or poke my friend Mikey?" A trusted infant care teacher becomes a secure base from which mobile infants can explore, checking back for reassurance and encouragement. Mobile infants develop feelings of confidence and competence as their infant care teachers share their pleasure in new discoveries and accomplishments. It is important for infant care teachers to remember that at this stage infants practice exploration but still need the security that trusted adults provide.

The Child

Mobile infants thrive on exploration and interaction. Mobility opens new worlds for infants. They can now move to what or whom they want by scooting; using their hands and bouncing forward; commando-crawling with stomach on the ground; one-legged stand-crawling;

crawling on all fours; walking with assistance; and, finally, toddling. They develop their large muscles as they creep, crawl, cruise, walk holding onto furniture or push toys, climb up onto couches and ramps, and descend stairs. Freedom to move about safely in an interesting, inviting environment is vital for these busy infants.

Mobile infants are fascinated by the daily activities of the other children and adults around them. Most likely they are found "in the fray" where they can observe what is going on and participate in their own way. They imitate actions they have seen, holding a comb to a doll's head, pretending to drink from a cup, and mimicking facial expressions of sadness or anger. The mental images mobile infants create of how things work and of sequences of peer and adult behaviors will become part of their rich repertoire of toddler play themes.

Adalia (4 months) had been a fussy baby. Her parents and infant care teacher had learned to respond quickly to the first signals of discomfort because her cries became unbearably loud within seconds. One day her father came into the center grinning. He reported with pride that when he awoke to Adalia's first morning call for a bottle, he had rushed to the crib, saying, "*Calladito bebé*. I know you're hungry. Papa's coming." Rather than the usual red-faced, screaming baby, he found Adalia with her thumb in her mouth, intently watching her kicking feet. At least for a moment, Adalia had learned to soothe and entertain herself. In their excitement, the infant care teacher and parent marveled at Adalia's new ability. Adalia did not know what she had done that was so exciting, but she enjoyed their enthusiasm!

This parent and infant care teacher clearly have a good relationship. One of the many rewards of this relationship is their shared enthusiasm for Adalia's accomplishments. Another is that through sharing their observations and thoughts, parents and infant care teachers can learn from each other. When one discovers a caregiving strategy that works, the other can try it too. This creates continuity and reinforces the baby's ability to anticipate effective adult responses to her needs.

Very young infants are frequently fussy as their central nervous system, digestive system, and other systems develop. Depending on how adults respond, infants learn very different lessons about themselves and their world. Responsive, consistent care helped Adalia trust that those who loved her would relieve her distress. When physically capable as well as emotionally and cognitively ready, she could begin to soothe her own physical discomfort, trusting that the sound of a familiar voice meant that relief was on its way.

Adalia's first successful attempt at self-soothing reflects multiple domains of learning. Physically, Adalia is using her thumb to satisfy the urge to suck and her kicking to distract her from her hunger. Cognitively, she can now associate the adult's voice with relief. Socially, she has taken an important step toward regulating or managing her reactions and will receive the rewards of happier and more relaxed caregiving. Emotionally, she has taken a giant step toward establishing trust and building a strong, secure attachment while also gaining a new sense of her own competence. When the infant care teacher understands such normal developmental challenges and achievements in the first 9 months of an infant's life, she can offer encouragement, insight, and support to both infants and family members. ✪

Mobile infants find their peers very interesting. Sometimes they smile and babble at each other socially. Other times they treat each other more like objects, experimenting to see what happens when they poke, prod, or crawl over them. They may choose a favorite friend to follow or imitate.

With mobile infants' new physical, cognitive, social, and emotional abilities come new discoveries and fears. They can look for a person who is momentarily out of sight, enjoy a game of peek-a-boo, and learn to wave bye-bye as they gain an understanding that people and objects exist even when they are out of sight. Although babies respond with differing degrees of intensity, on the basis of both their individual temperament and their experiences, almost all infants show some wariness of strangers during this period. A clown face, a firefighter in uniform, or a mask can be terrifying, especially if a trusted adult is not right there to provide comfort and reassurance.

Mobile infants express strong emotional ties to the adults they love, and they are acutely aware of their vulnerability when their loved ones are gone. A cherished object (a "lovey")—like a blanket, a piece of their parent's clothing, or a stuffed toy—can be very helpful as mobile infants navigate this very complicated and important emotional voyage toward independence.

Although new fears and anxieties are distressing to mobile infants and the adults who love them, these powerful feelings reflect new depths of understanding. Over these months, mobile infants are gradually developing an understanding that other people have their own experiences, feelings, and desires.

As they play, these young explorers can be totally absorbed. Opening and shutting, filling and dumping, and picking up and dropping are endlessly fascinating activities that challenge infants' mobility and dexterity as well as their ideas about objects and what they can do. They discover, test, and confirm that objects can be out of sight (inside a box or in a cabinet) and then found; that objects can be all together, separated into pieces, and then put together again; and that adults can be resources for reaching what has been dropped.

Photo credit: ©iStockphoto.com/Galina Barskaya

As they play and use their new physical skills, mobile infants learn the rudimentary rules of cause and effect. They learn to push buttons—on toys or a TV remote—and make interesting things happen. These infants use and manipulate tools (e.g., using a cup to scoop water). They also begin to group and compare objects, and may enjoy a simple stacking or nesting toy. They demonstrate a basic understanding of quantities of *more* and *less*. They work intently at simple problems, like fitting a lid on a pan or picking up a slippery ice cube or a strand of spaghetti.

Using language helps mobile infants stay connected with their infant care teachers over small distances. As these infants build their vocabularies, they listen to the sing-song rhythms, elevated pitch, and exaggerated emphasis on important words and sounds that most adults naturally use when talking with them. Reciprocal conversations take place with adults as the infant uses babbles, squeaks, and grunts. They begin to string together the familiar sounds of the languages in their environment into "expressive jargon" or "gibberish" that sounds a lot like sentences even though it does not contain meaningful words. The infants soon learn to respond to their name and to recognize the names of objects and people. They also learn to use simple gestures such as pointing, reaching up, pushing away, bouncing, and shaking their heads to signal their desires. Some will say their first words before their first birthdays; others will respond to words but be slower to use them.

Pierre looks tenderly at 8-month-old Yves, a little boy with Down syndrome, as he holds him in his lap and feeds him his bottle. After a few eager sucks, Yves takes the bottle in his hands, drinks for a bit, then pulls it out of his mouth, looks at Pierre, and smiles. "What a big boy!" he says in his home language. "I'll sing you a song while you drink your milk." Yves watches him and sucks contentedly as Pierre softly sings "Sur le Pont D'Avignon."

Illustration: Robert Saunders

Pierre is proud of Yves's ability to hold up his own bottle and feed himself. He knows, though, that Yves loves taking his bottle in Pierre's lap and still needs the security of his comforting arms and soothing voice. He also knows that propping a bottle for a baby or handing it to Yves to hold himself can contribute to gastrointestinal discomfort (from swallowing air and not being burped), tooth decay (when a child falls asleep with a bottle in his mouth or carries it around and takes frequent sucks), and even middle ear infections (when fluid pools at the back of the throat and gets into the Eustachian tubes). ⊙

Infant care teachers can encourage this interest in language by cuddling with one or two infants and reading simple board books to them several times each day. Pointing at pictures, naming people or objects, and making the sounds of animals in the pictures are good introductions to literacy and the importance of books.

Mobile infants love to play and interact with the caring adults in their lives, and can use their new language and motor skills to participate in baby games that are traditional in their culture(s). These games may include versions of peek-a-boo, hand-clapping rhymes, bouncing games, and games that involve pointing or gesturing. As they learn these routines, babies will come to anticipate the fun parts and will laugh and gesture at the appropriate times.

The mobile infant is both practicing independence and using new ways to stay connected to those he loves and trusts to protect him as he moves about on his own. Eye contact, vocalizing, and gesturing take on added importance as tools for maintaining that connection, although physical contact continues to be essential. A strong, loving relationship with a trusted adult gives the mobile infant the secure base from which he can explore his world.

The Infant Care Teacher

Mobile infants' new language, physical, and cognitive abilities may have a profound effect on relationships between them and their primary infant care teachers. Some infant care teachers miss the closeness of the young infant who depended so much on the teacher for meeting basic needs like food and comfort. An infant care teacher may reflect with her supervisor about how changes in the infant are affecting her. One infant care teacher mourned for one young infant she had loved. When he neared his first birthday she felt as though he was testing her every time he gleefully emptied a container of toys or toddled in the other direction when she called to him. The support of an understanding supervisor can be helpful in seeing such behavior from a developmental perspective.

The infant care teacher has a vital role in language development. Mobile infants are beginning to understand words. With an increased understanding of language, a new era of relatedness emerges. The earliest words children are exposed to often reflect the social environment, and these are usually the names of important adults, objects, and activities in their daily lives. Understanding of words is facilitated when infant care teachers slow down their speech and enunciate words clearly. Repeating names of people, objects, and actions; "narrating" what the infant is doing or seeing; giving the infant words for feelings; and using words from the infant's primary language are among the many ways that adults help babies learn new words.

An attentive infant care teacher can often interpret a child's actions and babbling and translate them into words. A teacher may say, "You want the truck" when she sees a child reach toward the shelf with the trucks and say, "tuk." This reinforces the infant's sense that she can communicate her needs and wishes to others. The joy in her eyes when her communication is understood, or when she hears the teacher use words spoken at home, reveals her excitement and eagerness to become competent in using language.

The care teacher has a special role in supporting infants who are dual-language learners. A mobile infant whose family speaks a different language than her teacher will feel supported in using her home language if her teacher learns some words of affection and songs from her family and gets simple picture books with captions in

Joanie (10 months) was in motion. She used a large yellow truck to pull herself up to a standing position, dropped to her knees, and crawled and scooted about the room. Then she crawled up the two-step platform and sat for a moment to survey the room. With her eyes, she called to Gina, her primary infant care teacher. Gina was with two other children, but Gina and Joanie smiled at each other. Gina called across the room, "You're so busy, Joanie! You go, girl!" Joanie rolled onto her tummy and slid down the carpeted steps where she sat and, again, looked over toward Gina.

When Gina picked up Malik, Joanie crawled across the floor, and pulled herself up holding Gina's knee, pouting. Gina stroked her hair, knelt down, and, put her free arm around Joanie, saying, "Hey girl, you want me to pick you up? I'm holding Malik, right now. How about we come watch you climb some more?" Joanie followed Gina's eyes to the steps and then crawled back to the platform. She looked back to be sure Gina had followed and called, "Ji! Ji! Ji!" in an excited voice.

This baby and her teacher have many ways of communicating. Eye contact is mutual and regular. Adult and child are in tune and check in regularly. A gesture of the arms, a sound, or a pout lets Gina know what Joanie needs. Gina responds with gestures (by putting her arm around Joanie to soothe her) and also puts Joanie's facial expressions into words. Joanie may not understand all of Gina's words, but she is beginning to understand many of them. She also knows from Gina's tone of voice and facial expressions that she can have her teacher's attention even when she has to share it with another baby.

This brief interaction reinforces Joanie's sense of herself as someone who is able to communicate, get what she needs, and control her intense feelings. It also lets her know that she is someone whose achievements are valued by an adult she loves and trusts. ✪

Illustration: Robert Saunders

Photo credit: Stephen Bobb

of all shapes and sizes are among the many things that fascinate mobile infants.

Infants with sensory or motor impairments or delays can be helped by infant care teachers who give them lots of opportunities to explore and experiment with objects and discover the results. Consultation with families or early interventionists may provide ideas for physical positioning or adapting toys and materials. Infant care teachers maintain the same emphasis on developing close relationships and supporting attachment and competence with infants with disabilities as with all infants.

Because mobile infants can be so easily overstimulated, sensitive adults will ensure that a good balance is maintained in the levels of intensity of play—from active to quiet to sleep. The infant care teacher sets up a developmentally appropriate environment that supports the infant's new mobility, but also provides protected areas for quieter play. Structures (e.g., low platforms, tunnels) invite the infant to pull herself up, take steps, climb up steps or risers, and crawl into partially enclosed spaces to gain new perspectives on the world. Spaces can be organized to invite specific types of activities. For example, a small nook, softly lit with cushions and books in pockets hung on the wall, says to the baby, "This is a place for quiet activities, books are special, and I am protected while I read."

the family's language. The message to the infant and her family is that their home language and culture are acknowledged and respected.

Infant care teachers sensitively support the mobile infant's peer interactions. Mobile infants tend to be very curious about other children and will grab at another's hair or pull his clothes with the same interest they show in sharing a picture book or crawling up a ramp side by side. Over time, an older infant may develop special affection for a same-aged playmate or older child and imitate her behavior, hand her a toy or a bite of food, or want to be near her. Because infants are not yet experienced in interacting with each other, they often require assistance from their infant care teachers so they do not unintentionally hurt each other.

Infant care teachers who regularly observe and document an infant's emerging interests and abilities can create inviting challenges that help mobile infants as they construct an understanding of the world. Mirrors, board books, sand and water, unusual textures, locks and latches, balls, push carts, doors, tubes, ramps, busy boards, and containers

Ensuring health and safety requires extra precautionary measures. Infant care teachers must check the environment regularly for potential dangers. Unlocked cabinets containing cleaning materials, uncovered electrical outlets, pot handles within the infant's reach, small objects, pieces of balloons, splinters, a purse left open, medications left out, and toys that are drooled on and shared are but a few of the long list of potential threats to an infant's health or safety. Infants who are just learning to toddle need room to roam, or to push a toy, without running over not-yet-mobile infants. Infant care teachers need to rapidly adapt to the changing needs of individual babies and the group as a whole.

The Infant Care Teacher/Family Alliance

The mobile infant, his family members, and his infant care teacher are entering a stage of development that is laced with complicated feelings about separation and attachment. There is much excitement and many challenges. At one moment, the baby is consumed with his own movement, crawling, scooting, or toddling off with abandon. In the next, he is fighting to keep the adult close and crying if left for a moment. Each partner in this triangle of relationships may experience different feelings at different times, each having his or her own complicated feelings about separation and attachment. Working together, parents, teachers, and supervisors can keep their focus on what is most important for the infant. They can identify and experiment with ways to maintain his sense of security in the child care setting, daily reinforcing his understanding that his family will be back, that they still love him, and that his infant care teacher will care for and protect him while separated from his family.

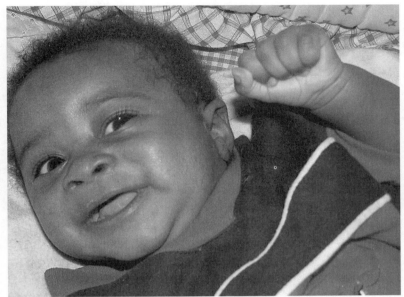

Photo credit: Marilyn Nolt

Many families place their infants in group care around the time they become mobile, often at a time when stranger wariness is at its height. At this time, the infant care teacher/family alliance becomes critical. An infant who sees that his mother or father trusts a new infant care teacher will relax in her presence and, with time,

As a young infant, Maya had moved easily through morning and evening transitions in her family child care, and a warm relationship had developed between Marina, Maya's mother, her partner Kristin, and Shanita, the family child care provider. At 16 months, however, Maya clung to Shanita one evening, unwilling to let her mother or Kristin hold her. The next evening, as Marina and Kristin arrived while Maya was playing, they were greeted with her tears.

Shanita spoke to them about Maya's tears. "You know, this can feel terrible to parents, but it happens all of the time with children. Now she understands that you are still out there somewhere when you go. Her tears may be telling you she is confused and mad that you left her. This is really normal. Or she may be telling you that she wants some time to make the transition from child care to home and wants you to spend some time with her playing in her space before you go home." Marina and Kristin thought about this. Kristin said, "I guess this is a part of separations we just didn't see." Marina sat on the floor with Maya, looked intently into her eyes, and said in a soft voice: "Hey baby, let's play." Maya, with bright eyes, repeated "Mama play? Mama play?"

Shanita, knowing how different infants work through the strong emotions associated with managing different relationships and dealing with separations from loved ones, responds empathically by telling the parents that what is happening is normal and does not mean that the baby now prefers her provider to her parents. By doing so, she avoids the development of jealousy that might undermine her relationship with Marina or Kristin. Shanita offers several ways to understand Maya's behavior and some strategies they can use to work through the transition together. Shanita is using her knowledge and skills to help both parents and baby negotiate what will be one of many emotionally charged moments in parenting. ✪

become secure enough to leave his parent with less distress. The relationships among adults constantly influence the child's experience with the adults.

Open and frequent communication is needed to assure continuity between the family and infant care teacher. Parents will want to know not just about the baby's eating and sleeping patterns, but also about her development and discoveries. The baby's milestones—first words, first steps, or first drink from a cup—are exciting to both parents and infant care teachers. Often a sensitive teacher will resist the temptation to tell a child's family about a really big accomplishment until the parents have the opportunity to see it for themselves. Instead, the teacher might cue the parent to watch for the big moment: "She's almost walking. I think she might take some steps this week!"

Because parents are highly sensitive to how a care teacher may feel about their baby, it is useful to genuinely and explicitly comment at times on how good-natured, lovable, serious, giggly, alert, or fun their baby is. It is reassuring to parents to hear how it is for the care teacher to be with their baby.

Negotiations with families must be guided by the infant care teacher's commitment to reaching a mutual under-standing. A mutual understanding of the baby's use of the word *no* is a good example. While mobile infants might be encouraged by the infant care teacher to use no as a tool for self-defense and a statement of independ-ence, many families do not believe that it is appropriate to allow a young child to say no. In some cultures, such statements of independence, especially when directed toward an adult, are viewed as highly inappropriate. Cultural beliefs and rules about infants' self-feeding, being "loud," and moving without restraint also vary.

The infant care teacher who anticipates that cultural and child-rearing beliefs will differ among families is prepared for open communication in an equitable and nonjudgmental way. If their beliefs conflict, a care teacher and family can try to find a mutually acceptable approach by talking over a range of strategies. The skilled infant care teacher appreciates that being a competent professional requires the ability to listen carefully, explore the parent's perspective fully, and to work toward compromise and agreement. Some of these differences can be very difficult to resolve. Whatever feelings are aroused in caring for a young child,

Photo credit: Stephen Bobb

it is critical for there to be a strong alliance between the infant care teacher and parent so that they can support and share insights with each other.

Toddlers (16 to 36 Months)

Toddlers are primarily concerned with developing an understanding of who they are. Beginning at around 18 months, identity becomes the dominant theme for them. Developing this sense of self has a lot to do with their desire and drive for independence and control. Whether toddlers are still teetering with a wide-based gait, confi-dently getting around on two legs, or standing only with assistance, they are busy "standing up for themselves." They use their rapidly developing communication skills to indicate their desires and refuse what they do not want at the moment. As their social awareness expands, they pick up cultural messages about who they are and how they should be. Their most frequent statements are likely to include "No," "Mine," "Why," and "Me do it."

Of course, the sense of security that began to develop in the earliest months and the desire to explore (with increasing purposefulness) continue. Toddler care teachers can help toddlers find appropriate ways to assert themselves by supporting their individuality, giving them choices whenever possible, and introducing social guidelines. Toddlers work very hard to understand social rules and get things right. The toddler care teacher fosters cooperation and facilitates the toddler's development of a strong sense of self. A well-designed environment offers toddlers many chances to be in control as they participate in group play, fantasy play, and independent activities.

The Child

Young toddlers are busy exploring the world from their new, upright vantage point. At the same time they are, quite literally, gaining a new sense of themselves as either a "big boy" or a "big girl." They do the things they see the important people in their lives do, or at least they try. Reassured by the presence of a loved family member or toddler care teacher, they busily explore and construct an understanding of the world.

Once toddlers master walking, their motor skills grow by leaps and bounds. They learn to jump, tiptoe, march, throw and kick a ball, and make a riding toy go by pushing with their feet or perhaps even pedaling. Toddlers love to tear paper, pull all of the toys off of a shelf at once, tromp through every puddle they can find, carry as much as they can hold from one place to another, and make lots of noise. Excited by their new motor abilities, they plunge ahead full speed before figuring out how to stop.

Toddlers are especially intrigued with the daily activities they see adults engage in and watch intently as grown-ups go about daily tasks of cooking, cleaning, building, and fixing. These experiences provide fuel for "stories" that toddlers tell over and over in their play, both with and without words. Instead of just pushing a truck, for example, they may drive it to a spot, fill it with sand, and then drive it to a new location to dump the sand. They might also use miniature figures to replay a frightening event, such as being barked at by a big dog or getting a "boo-boo."

Toddlers are fascinated by words. They constantly ask "Wha's dat?" and repeat words and phrases they hear. They enjoy following simple instructions, and, as they

Kirsty, a 22-month-old who was just beginning to put words together, lived in a rural area. One winter day a fox trotted past the living room window. Kirsty's father pointed excitedly as it ran out of sight, then showed Kirsty the tracks in the snow. "See fox" said Kirsty the next morning. "Yes," replied her father, "we saw a fox." "Feet," said Kirsty. Her father elaborated. "Its feet made tracks in the snow," and Kirsty repeated "snow." Over the next several days, Kirsty told the fox story dozens of times, helped by her mother and father, and then by her clued-in toddler care teacher. Kirsty's few contributions—"See fox," "feet," and "snow"—were soon supplemented with "run," "fast," "tracks," "tail," and "red" as the story grew more elaborate.

Illustration: Robert Saunders

Kirsty is as excited as her parents and toddler care teacher by her new ability to use words to share a memory. Her father's delight encourages Kirsty to tell the story over and over again. Over time, her father scaffolds Kirsty's learning by adding just a bit more. Because Kirsty's parents and toddler care teacher talk frequently about the skills that Kirsty is working on and the new interests she is showing, Kirsty's mother and then her toddler care teacher are able to pick up with Kirsty where she and her father left off. ✪

learn to talk, even give instructions to themselves. For example, a toddler may tell herself "No, no, no" or "Hot," as she tries to contain her exuberance. Toddlers can also use words to express strong feelings and to evoke what is not present. A child may repeat a phrase like "Daddy come back" in a ritualistic way to comfort herself when feeling the sadness of separation, to reassure herself that the separation is not permanent.

Toddlers love to hear stories about themselves and the people and things they love. They also love books—especially sturdy ones they can easily manipulate with clear pictures and lots of things to do—textures to feel, holes to peek through or poke fingers into, sounds to make, and actions to imitate. Illustrations of familiar objects and activities (or photo albums of favorite people), and simple, poetic text in their home language, invite toddlers to join in the telling of the story.

Photo credit: Stephen Bobb

They do this in many ways: by repeating words and phrases, making appropriate sounds for animals and machines, naming or pointing out pictures and details upon request, asking questions, and turning the pages. Many classic stories for toddlers involve searching for a mother, running away and coming back, being lost and found again, or doing something bad and being forgiven. These themes resonate with the toddler's ongoing struggles to balance his desires for independence and closeness, for being "big" and being a "baby."

As toddlers' verbal skills expand, so does their ability to use objects, to put together a series of actions in play, and to remember events for later reenactment. Adults are especially valued play partners because they can keep the story going, as they respond to the child's lead by adding missing words or by suggesting next steps or new elements. An adult can support a toddler's need to repeat the same story over and over again, encourage her to do more of the storytelling each time, and help her to extend or elaborate on her story. Peers are also highly valued play partners as they heighten the emotional tone of play, take different roles, or share ideas for solving problems.

Through their experimentation with objects, language, and social interactions, toddlers enter a new phase of cognitive growth. They love to divide objects into cate-

gories by shape, size, color, or type. What toddlers are learning through play, observation, and exploration is truly amazing. They might call anything with four legs and a tail a "doggie" or remember which blocks go with the shape puzzle. They might line up rubber animals according to their height, find all of the cows, or even pair a big animal with a little one and call them "mommy and baby." They are developing increasingly sophisticated mental representations of the real world and mastering them through using them in play.

Toddlers' social awareness is far more complex than that of infants. They actively seek out their friends and especially enjoy imitating each other's behavior and engaging in group activities like a simple game of follow the leader. Toddlers will work together to carry a large object, dig a hole in the sandbox, or make a bed for a doll. As their language and social skills become more sophisticated, they may begin to take on simple pretend play roles like doctor and patient or parent and child. They choose friends who share their interests and will play with them. Over time, in pairs or small groups, toddler friends develop their own rituals, favorite games, and deepening affections and attachments.

Even very young toddlers are capable of empathy and touching kindness in their own ways. Their interactions with children and adults may at times seem very sophisticated, for example, when they imitate a gentle adult and comfort a hurt friend or tenderly pat a baby. At other times, fatigue, anxiety, or other distress overwhelms them, and they burst into tears or full-blown tantrums.

As they increasingly tune in to the social world, toddlers become particularly interested in their bodies and those of others. They begin to learn what it means to be a boy or a girl: both physically, when they notice differences in their body parts, and socially, especially as they notice the differences in gender roles within their culture. Some of this awareness develops as learning to use the toilet becomes an important issue during the third year of life, especially as children see peers giving up diapers. Toilet learning should begin when the child shows signs of interest and readiness. Adults need to follow the child's lead as she shows a desire for privacy when having a bowel movement in a diaper, expresses discomfort in a filled diaper, and shows interest in toileting.

Toddlers' exploration of the social world often involves conflict. The most basic conflict being about "what is mine" and "what is yours." Toddlers react impulsively, but their feelings of empathy blossom as they negotiate these con-flicts and see that other people have feelings too. They are beginning to understand that other people's thoughts and feelings may differ from their own, such as "I want to pull this lamp down but Mama doesn't want me to." Some-times they try to do things they are told not to, just to see the other person's reactions. Toddlers can easily fall into despair at not getting what they want or when they sense the displeasure of a beloved adult; just as easily, they can react with true generosity and warmth. Through such experiences, toddlers build a sense of themselves as social beings: competent, cooperative, and emotionally connected.

The Toddler Care Teacher

The toddler care teacher wears many hats. She is likely to be teacher, comforter, referee, diaper changer, playmate, and storyteller—all in the course of a day. Remaining emotionally available in so many roles to several toddlers at once is challenging. Coteachers, parents, and supervisors each become members of the nesting of adult relationships that support the infant or toddler care teacher to remain present and positive with the children. The toddlers, in turn, observe these adult relationships and learn how to build strong, positive relationships with other people.

All of the children in Lei-Ann's family child care home are busy "writing letters." It started when Rosa was sick one day, and Nadia wanted to send her a get well card. Nadia, at 5, knew that a proper letter required a stamp and had to be put in a mailbox, so Lei-Ann gave her an envelope and a stamp and helped her write Rosa's address. Then the whole group took a walk to the mailbox. Noticing that her toddlers were fascinated with the idea that a letter could disappear into a box and end up at someone's house, Lei-Ann made up some address labels and return address stickers so the children could send each other mail: both within the group by putting them in a special box and, for really special messages, through the U.S. postal service.

Illustration: Robert Saunders

Toddlers benefit from opportunities to imitate reading and writing in their pretend play. They can participate in these grown-up activities by scribbling "notes," making pictures and books, dictating words and seeing how they appear in print, and "reading" their messages. ✪

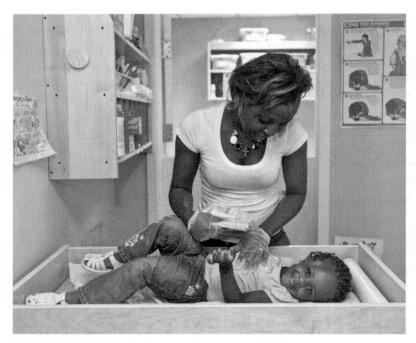

Photo credit: Stephen Bobb

manage her impulses by giving her strategies such as "touch gently" or "use your words." They also know when a toddler is acting out deep emotions and give her the space—and support—to work them through.

One of the great benefits of group care is the ongoing opportunities to be with peers as this provides the invaluable opportunity for children to learn the social rules and to get along with others—a critical life skill. The toddler care teacher helps the child understand how he is seen by others and to consider how his actions affect others. As the child becomes aware of other people's thoughts and feelings, the care teacher helps him begin to understand how the experiences of others may also affect his feelings. On a practical level, the care teacher must be prepared to prevent injuries and handle conflicts as toddlers learn to defend themselves, share, and cooperate with others. She gives them opportunities to help others, and takes advantage of unplanned encounters that allow the toddler to show his competence.

Part of the care teacher's role in supporting the child's growing identity includes showing him how positively he is seen in her eyes and helping him understand how he affects others. She recognizes that while striving to be independent and self-reliant, toddlers count on the understanding and watchfulness of the adults who love them. Whether setting limits for safety or joining in exploring a puddle, the responsive toddler care teacher gives the consistent message to each toddler that "you are loveable and capable."

Even with consistent routines, conflicts are inevitable as toddlers learn the rules of their culture in ways that keep their dignity intact. Simple explanations help toddlers understand and accept necessary warnings and limits: "that will break," "hold my hand so you don't fall," or "it hurts your friend when you pull his hair." Toddlers need consistent limits by adults who can be counted on and who mean what they say. Clear rules and limits enable toddlers to learn to make good decisions.

Skilled toddler care teachers offer toddlers many opportunities to do things for themselves, both as individuals and as members of the group. They equip the setting with materials that facilitate self-help skills, such as small

Adults who know a toddler well can help her cope with frustrations and disappointments. These trusted adults can recognize her signs of stress and may prevent her losing control. At the same time, they can help the child learn to

Photo credit: Stephen Bobb

Donna held Haniya, a toddler with cerebral palsy, so that Haniya could hold her hands under the faucet. Jonathan came in from the adjoining play area to wash his hands before snack. Donna said to Jonathan, "Please turn on the faucet for Haniya." Jonathan did. Haniya glanced at him and gave a faint smile. She stuck her hands under the faucet of running water, seeming to enjoy the warm feeling on her hands. Jonathan stuck his hands under the water also and they splashed the water together. Haniya's smile filled her face and they laughed. Jonathan pushed the soap dispenser for Haniya and then for himself. Donna helped both children wash between their fingers then gave Haniya a paper towel to give Jonathan, who took it gently from her saying, "Tank you Haniya."

This care teacher knows how to extend this moment of intimacy and cooperation between these two toddlers, letting each use his or her skills to help the other. She only intervenes to be sure that each child learns proper hand washing. Thus, good habits of personal hygiene, essential for reducing the spread of infection in child care settings, are taught within the context of interaction and cooperation. The bathroom is also set up to offer such opportunities. It allows both children to reach the sink, soap, and paper towels on their own. Teaching proper personal hygiene is critical as toddlers are increasingly capable of doing things by themselves and especially when learning to use the toilet. What could be better than the magic of one toddler helping another and showing off new competence at proper hand washing? ⊗

pitchers and serving utensils or easy-to-put-on smocks. They give toddlers opportunities to help with tasks like setting the table and cleaning up. Participating in these activities increases the toddler's sense of himself as a competent person with valuable contributions to make. Sensitive teachers make themselves available without intruding and offer hints and suggestions that provide just enough help for the toddler to feel successful. In this case, the teacher is primarily observing and supporting the child's intentions. This may seem disorganized to parents in some cultural communities. At the same time, teachers recognize that the value families place on developing self-help skills varies from culture to culture, especially around meal times. Some parents may be concerned about spills or wasted food or feel that feeding and dressing children are important ways in which adults show their love and care. It would be helpful to discuss parents' feelings and ideas about self-direction and how the infant care teacher is helping the children.

Photo credit: Stephen Bobb

Toddler care teachers do a lot of talking and asking. They also do a lot of listening. As they talk with toddlers individually and in small groups, teachers often wonder with children. "What do you think this book is about?" "What will happen when we mix these colors?" "How can we help our friend who is crying?" Recognizing that 2-year-olds are beginning to develop ideas about how things work, their teachers provide lots of opportunities to explore interesting phenomena, make predictions, and talk about what happened. Toddlers who hear and practice lots of rich and varied language develop extensive vocabularies. They learn to "use their words" to play with their friends, control their own behavior, ask interesting questions, and solve problems. Skilled toddler care teachers talk with toddlers about the past and the future as well as the present. They expand upon children's ideas, not only by phrasing them in complete sentences, but also by introducing new words and concepts and asking questions that make children think. A skilled toddler care

Photo credit: Stephen Bobb

teacher is also aware that when a dual-language learner toddler's attention is on trying to understand the mainstream language, he may be "silent" for a period of time and it does not necessarily mean he has a language delay. She would recognize and acknowledge his attempts at communicating through nonverbal gestures or facial expressions.

A skillful care teacher shares books with toddlers both individually and in small groups and both spontaneously and at predictable times within the daily routine. She might read a special story to a toddler who needs calming or comforting, help a child share a book from home with a small group of friends, or introduce a book that recognizes a child's special interest. She might also have regular "story times" early in the day and just before nap, when children who are interested can listen to a story together. It is important to note that toddlers are not "required" to join the circle or stay for the whole story; other quiet activities can also be available that will spark their curiosity or help them make the transition from lunch or playtime to nap.

Balancing the needs of individuals with those of the group presents daily challenges because some toddlers may still have individual patterns of eating, sleeping, active play, and need for quiet engagement with a favorite adult or an

intriguing activity. At the same time, they are drawn to each other and can enjoy simple small group activities that provide opportunities for imitation, parallel play, or group participation. A consistent but flexible routine gives toddlers a sense of security and creates opportunities for a variety of stimulating group activities while still accommodating individual needs. The toddler care teacher may need to help toddlers with special needs to stay close to other children and participate in their play.

A predictable routine allows toddler care teachers to plan a mix of play opportunities that balance physical activities like running, climbing, and dancing with quieter, focused activities that involve rich conversation. Toddler care teachers frequently join children in their pretend play, following a child's lead and helping her to tell her story. They balance new toys, books, songs, and activities with old favorites, giving children time to consolidate new skills and vocabulary while also fueling their curiosity. Children's emerging interests—expressed in questions, worries, play themes, favored activities, and requests—

Photo credit: Stephen Bobb

During a walk in the park, Richie (32 months) picked up a large branch that had fallen from a tree. As Amy began her customary speech about leaving sticks on the ground because they might poke someone, Richie explained that the stick was his cello. He ran his hand across the branch singing "De-dah," tapping his toes, and moving his head to the beat. "Okay," Amy said, "we'll take the cello back with us." Richie's father, a musician, had recently moved out of the house, and Richie was struggling with how thoroughly everything in his life seemed to change. Amy wondered if music might be a connection with his father. When the group got back to the center, Richie, sitting on a milk crate and using a wooden spoon for a bow, gave the group a concert with his cello. It was the beginning of a ritual. Every afternoon after nap, children would help get the cello out from under the red sofa, and there would be a concert as Richie re-created a connection with his father.

Illustration: Robert Saunders

In a few critical minutes during an ordinary outing, this sensitive toddler care teacher draws on many areas of knowledge, skill, and experience. As Richie picks up a stick, Amy's practiced vigilance about children's safety and health lead her to intervene quickly. But as Richie explains (his experience with Amy must have taught him that she will listen), Amy slows down. Her general knowledge of toddler development helps her to appreciate Richie's emerging capacities to express himself through language and dramatic play. Her awareness of Richie's specific situation helps her to grasp the emotional meaning of "the cello" for Richie and to find a way to support this young child's courageous effort to maintain a connection with his father. Amy adapts rapidly. She agrees to carry the stick while simultaneously protecting the group's safety, the group's respect for safety rules, Richie's dignity, and her individual relationship based on trust with Richie. Once back at the center, Amy creates an opportunity for Richie to use his creativity not only to master his own pain but also to contribute to the shared life of the group.

In conversations with Richie's mother and father, Amy will listen for opportunities to tell them about the cello concerts and then listen carefully for clues to help her support the whole family during their difficult transition. She may share books and pictures of musical instruments with Richie and his classmates, as well as read them stories in which characters stay emotionally connected while they are physically apart. She knows that sharing favorite books with her and his father and mother can help Richie maintain strong connections with all of the people he loves.

shape a "curriculum" as the teacher plans from her observation and documentation of the children's activities.

Unfortunately, many infants and toddlers experience the trauma of fighting in the family, divorce, chronic illness, death of a family member, or violence in the community. Their ability to overcome the hurt and fear depends, in large measure, on whether they are secure in relationships with a few caring adults who understand what they have

experienced. Teachers try to provide these children with extra attention, tolerance, and appreciation for their feelings and help them to manage them. The care teacher's greatest assets in dealing with such situations are her responsiveness to the child and her commitment to being a resource and support to the family.

Photo credit: Stephen Bobb

The Toddler Care Teacher/Family Alliance

Caring for toddlers can be challenging for adults. The toddler's bouts of frustration can be emotionally draining while the pure joy of discovery is heartwarming. It is difficult at times to understand that as he pushes away and hurls himself into action, the toddler is still very much in need of his special adults and the secure base they offer.

A healthy toddler's inner world is filled with conflicting feelings: independence and dependence, pride and shame, confidence and doubt, fear and omnipotence, and hostility and intense love. These feelings challenge parents' and toddler care teachers' resourcefulness and knowledge, as they work together to provide toddlers with emotional security. "What is this child trying to tell us with his behavior?" is a question that parents and toddler care teachers share and can help each other answer. When care teachers and families keep each other informed of the toddler's emerging interests and the significant events in her life, they can help the toddler put her knowledge, feelings, and questions into words that, in turn, help parents and teachers better support her.

A child's sense of identity is rooted in his family and community. Each toddler brings a world of family-based learning into a group care situation. His words, patterns of movement, preferences for foods and music, play themes, and ways of asking questions and expressing emotions reflect his home experiences. When toddlers see that care teachers and families are comfortable with each other, they observe communication and respect for both home and group care. Parents and teachers with a good relationship can help each other better understand the toddler as they share their experiences, insights, and encouragement. They also share their pleasure in just who this child is, his special ways of being and doing. This provides a sturdy, positive background if concerns arise about the child's development in a particular area or in the persistence of troubling behaviors. The parents and teachers have a relationship to draw on if they need to seek additional consultation or early intervention assessment and work together to follow up on any recommendations.

Communication between families and toddler care teachers builds mutual understanding and creates continuity between home and child care. It is particularly essential when there are cultural or language differences. If the

Photo credit: Stephen Bobb

child's primary toddler care teacher does not speak his home language, there are strategies available to meet the challenge. For example, bilingual, bicultural members of the family's community can be recruited to help the toddler care teacher learn at least a few important words, interpret during family–toddler care teacher conferences, and explain important program policies. There are many ways to show respect and help the family feel welcome in the child care setting.

Toddlers whose home language is different from that used in the group care environment need to hear their own language spoken and see it written. These opportunities help them build on their home language while learning English. In valuing the child's home language, his teachers reinforce his pride in family and community as well as

his feelings of competence in mastering the challenges of a culturally and linguistically different environment.

The issues of identity, interdependence, and control that are paramount for toddlers can hold different meaning and value for different cultures and familial beliefs. Some families encourage early independence in feeding and dressing, whereas others see these caretaking activities as essential ways that adults show love throughout the early childhood years. Some families are comfortable with messy play and are amused when their toddlers cover themselves with dirt or food as they try to do things themselves. Others are uncomfortable with and work hard to limit these behaviors. Some families have firm ideas about gender roles and do not want their boys playing with dolls or their girls playing with trucks. Others

Haida, an 18-month-old from Iran, was starting child care in the United States. For the first week Haida's grandmother accompanied her to the child care program to help ease the transition. As long as her grandmother was there, Haida seemed to be making a good adjustment, although she seemed a bit wary of Jennifer, her new teacher.

Haida's other teacher, Paul, had been out sick, and came back to work on the first day that Haida arrived without her grandmother. He found Haida sitting in Jennifer's lap crying. Paul had prepared for the arrival of this new child and learned a few words of Farsi. "Salaan," he greeted Haida. "Halet chatore?" Haida did not need words in any language to answer that she was fine. She reached her arms up to Paul, accepted his big hug, and stayed near him for the rest of the day. Paul became Haida's primary toddler care teacher; Haida's instant and ongoing affection for Paul soon helped her feel comfortable with Jennifer as well.

Illustration: Robert Saunders

Although Paul did not share Haida's culture or language, just the fact that he knew a few familiar words was enough to help Haida feel safe in a very stressful situation. Ideally, child care programs for infants and toddlers would include teachers who speak their home languages and are intimately familiar with their cultures. A toddler who is not speaking in sentences yet will still prefer the words she hears at home. Although she may learn a new language rapidly in a child care setting, her home language will continue to be a vital part of her identity. When a child's primary toddler care teacher does not speak her home language, even a few words can help—especially if they are words of friendly greeting, endearment, or the names of the toddler's favorite things. ✪

Photo credit: Stephen Bobb

might feel. The toddler care teacher prepares her children for new experiences with other children. As they read favorite books together, she takes the opportunity to talk with them about the feelings, choices, and actions of the characters.

For families who are struggling with poverty, low literacy levels, family disruptions or violence, or adjustment to a new community and culture—and for every family dealing with the everyday challenges of parenting a toddler—the community that forms around a shared child care setting can be a vital support. Potluck suppers, special celebrations, parents' nights out, and family reading parties help build a community that enjoys their young children together and supports them as they grow.

are worried when they see their children fall into stereotypical gender patterns and deliberately encourage a wider range of activities. In some families, toys belong to individual children who can choose whether and when to share. In others, toys and other objects belong to everyone and sharing is expected. Talking these issues through with parents when they arise, both in one-to-one conferences and in parent group meetings, can assure that deeply held beliefs are respected, differences accommodated, and necessary compromises made so that all children feel at home in the group.

In some areas there are no compromises. Some parents believe that toddlers should work out conflicts for themselves, and that it is alright for a toddler to hit back.

In a group setting, it is never right, nor is it ever acceptable, to hit, shake, or shame a child, or to encourage or permit one child to hurt another—even in self-defense. This does not mean, however, that toddler care teachers should always intervene in children's quarrels. Often, children will solve the problem themselves when they are not competing for a grown-up's attention. The toddler care teacher who knows her charges well is alert to signs of stress and frustration, and can help children "use their words" and devise a solution before a conflict escalates. She also finds time to teach cooperation skills as she engages in pretend play, explores, and wonders with children about how other children or characters in books

When families and teachers work together, each family's expertise can enrich the group experience. Families can be invaluable resources for each other, sharing information, trading parenting ideas, and helping each other in times of need. Family friendships formed during toddler play dates and child care events often last a lifetime; teachers can play an important role in making and supporting these links.

Good relationships among the adults who love and care for toddlers help them deal with their inevitable emotional ups and downs. The adults can share strategies for helping the toddler manage or avoid tantrums, prepare for new situations, take on a challenge like toilet learning, and practice safe behavior. Toddlers need continuity between the expectations of their families and those of their care teachers. However, they can cope with different approaches as long as the adults work together to make the differences clear and when they show support of each other.

When parents and care teachers inform each other about the issues that arise in the group care setting and at home, they can share techniques for helping children express their feelings and practice positive ways to handle challenging social situations. Parents and care teachers who have built a good relationship can help each other better understand and help the toddler as they share their experiences and insights and offer each other encouragement.

CHAPTER 2

Components of Quality Infant–Toddler Child Care

Ultimately, the quality of a child's experience in any one moment depends on the infant toddler care teacher's response to what she observes. For example, a toddler rushing to hug another in welcome causes them both to fall to the floor. Neither is hurt. One toddler care teacher may recognize the friendly intent and laughter and say, "What good friends you are! You're so happy to see each other! Everybody okay?" Another toddler care teacher may respond by pulling them apart and saying, "You're going to hurt each other. Stop that." The first response expresses approval of the children's actions and intentions; the second implies disapproval of both.

However, the care teacher's responses in the moment are, in many ways, the result of how well the program has established systems to assure quality. Studies of group care over the past several decades have identified several components of quality that have the greatest effect on children benefiting and thriving from their experience within groups (Clarke-Stewart, Vandell, Burchinal, O'Brien, & McCartney, 2002; National Institute of Child Health and Human Development [NICHD] & Early Child Care Research Network [ECCRN], 1996; NICHD & ECCRN, 2000; Phillipsen, Burchinal, Howes, & Cryer, 1997; Vandell & Wolfe, 2002). Some of these are the responsibility of the care teacher, others depend on program management. The primary elements of quality are as follows:

1. Promotion of health and well-being

2. Developmentally appropriate practice

3. Program structures that support relationships

4. Family and community partnerships

5. Responsible financial and program management

Promotion of Health and Well-Being

Keeping infants and toddlers healthy and safe is the first priority for group care. It requires a combination of reducing the risk of illness or injury with active promotion of exercise and good nutrition.

Immature immune systems make infants and toddlers susceptible to infectious diseases. In addition, their emerging mobility and curiosity put them at risk for injury. A basic challenge in the group care of infants and toddlers is creating a safe and sanitary environment that is interesting to the children and can be maintained efficiently so that infant care teachers have enough time for intimate, responsive interaction with each infant and toddler. Each state's licensing requirements articulate a basic set of health and safety regulations.

Achieving safe and healthy practices requires

- Careful planning of areas for food preparation and diapering/toileting, including adequate storage cabinets easily accessible to adults;

- Detailed and scrupulously maintained health policies (including emergency, injury, and health procedures as well as clear attendance guidelines related to both mild and highly contagious illnesses) and child and staff health records (including health history, evidence of required immunizations for children and staff and of annual staff physicals and Mantoux tuberculosis tests, health and injury reports, and posted information about care of children with allergies or special medical needs);

- Concise but thorough policies and procedures that enable efficient use of staff time;

- Orientation, in-service training, and ongoing supervision specifically of hand-washing, sanitation, proper handling and storage of disinfectants, and use of gloves;

- Time for infant care teachers to meet to share current health and safety information, concerns, and problems and to generate solutions;

- Daily communication between family members and infant care teachers, with daily record keeping on each child and special reports to all families when an infectious disease is present or a safety issue (such as lead poisoning risks in the community) has arisen;

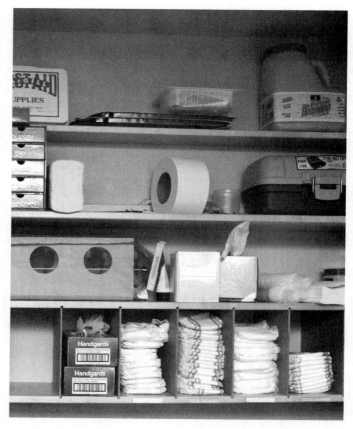

Photo credit: Stephen Bobb

Illustration: Robert Saunders

It was a cold, gray March day and almost every baby in Brenda's care had a runny nose, a cough, and a fussy attitude. She did not feel that well herself. It seemed as though winter would never end and the babies would never stop passing this virus around. Yolanda, her director, stopped in and offered to help. After awhile, Yolanda said, "Oh, Brenda. Another round of colds! You poor thing! There must be something we can do to help stop spreading this virus. Let's look back over our sanitizing and hand-washing policies and see if we're doing them exactly right."

Yolanda knew that under the pressure of daily routines, an infant care teacher might have a difficult time implementing all of the health and safety policies—with potentially disastrous results. Training, supervision, and monitoring of the health and safety procedures all need to be in place to assure that policies and procedures are being followed. ✪

- Constant monitoring of all children's activities and elimination of potential hazards; and

- Knowledge of and collaboration with community health and safety resources.

Of course, policies alone do not guarantee a safe and healthy environment. Infant and toddler care teachers need training and supervision in these practices, and the program needs a process of ongoing monitoring to assure the procedures are followed.

Every care teacher should be trained in pediatric first aid and rescue breathing and maintain certification according to state regulations (e.g., retrain/test every 3 years). Emergency evacuation procedures must be planned carefully and practiced regularly. Care teachers should also know how to minimize the common health hazards of their occupation, such as easily transmitted infections and injuries resulting from lifting children.

Photo credit: Stephen Bobb

Recommended Policies and Procedures

Caring for Our Children, The National Health and Safety Performance Standards: Guidelines for Out-of-Home Child Care Programs (American Academy of Pediatrics, 2002) provides detailed information on how to promote health and prevent injury or infection. The *Standards* recommend that policies, procedures, and training be in place for the following:

- Environments that encourage large muscle activity and daily outdoor play;

- Daily health checks, tracking, and documentation of well-baby care; responsive individualized schedules for sleeping and eating as well as regular oral hygiene routines;

- Sanitary toileting and diapering procedures;

- Hand-washing;

- Sanitation and disinfection of toys, surfaces, and potty chairs;

- Safety concerning tobacco and other substances, exposure to pets, bodies of water;

- Daily safety checks of the environment;

- Emergency procedures including first aid and CPR, evacuation, and transportation to a hospital;

- Reporting of child abuse, neglect, or exploitation;

- Care of children with specific medical conditions;

- Exclusion of children with contagious diseases;

- Medication administration; and

- Nutrition and food service.

Photo credit: Stephen Bobb

All programs benefit from having a health consultant (e.g., a nurse or pediatrician) with expertise in serving infants and toddlers in groups. They can help create and review policies, advise on potential infectious diseases, provide information to parents, and confer with staff when concerns arise. Environmental health specialists, playground designers, and other professionals can offer expertise on outdoor and indoor equipment safety, traffic, and fire safety. A mental health consultant can be invaluable in helping staff foster the healthy social and emotional development of children and families while also protecting their own emotional well-being.

Developmentally Appropriate Practice

In their position paper on developmentally appropriate practice, The National Association for the Education of Young Children (NAEYC; 2006) describes developmentally appropriate practice as a result of the process of professionals making decisions about the well-being and education of children that are based on at least three important kinds of information or knowledge:

1. *What is known about child development and learning*—knowledge of age-related human characteristics that permits general predictions within an age range about what activities, materials, interactions, or experiences will be safe, healthy, interesting, achievable, and also challenging to children.

2. *What is known about the strengths, interests, and needs of each individual child in the group* to be able to adapt for and be responsive to inevitable individual variation.

3. *Knowledge of the social and cultural contexts in which children live* to ensure that learning experiences are meaningful, relevant, and respectful for the participating children and their families (NAEYC, 1996, p. 5).

These practices are often referred to as (a) age appropriate, (b) individually appropriate, and (c) culturally and linguistically appropriate practices.

The promotion of health and safety goes beyond preventing illness and accidents to that of promoting healthy habits. Recent research on childhood obesity suggests that active lifestyles and healthy eating habits are established in infancy (Deiner & Qiu, 2007). Infant–toddler care teachers model and offer nutritious food choices, carry out oral health routines for babies and help toddlers with tooth brushing, and observe the Back to Sleep procedures for reducing the risk of sudden infant death syndrome (SIDS). It is difficult to imagine infants and toddlers not moving, but the use of swings, car seats, and other "containing" equipment, along with the increasingly common use of television to occupy babies, may be creating even sedentary toddlers!

Programs should be aware of and know how to use the health resources that are available in their community. Families may need help identifying a medical home and keeping current with immunizations and well-baby checkups. State and local health departments often have resources to offer in a variety of languages that can help children and families get the ongoing health care they need. Given the low wages and benefits typical in the early childhood field, infant and toddler care teachers must also be resourceful in order to find good health care for themselves and maintain healthy routines.

Photo credit: Stephen Bobb

Age Appropriate Practice

Knowledge of child development provides the basis for age appropriate practice. Although development occurs in unique ways in each child, there are predictable patterns of development that we expect to see within certain age ranges. Guided by their knowledge of children's general skills and interests, infant toddler care teachers are constantly making decisions about their own interactions, the activities they offer, and how they set up the environment. Infant–toddler care teachers need the following:

• Training in infant toddler development,

• Skills to create an environment that supports thoughtful observation and reflection,

The 2-year-olds in Aileen's family child care home had developed a disturbing new game: cooking the baby dolls in the oven. Aileen wondered whether they had overheard the phrase "a bun in the oven" and were acting out what they thought it meant or whether there was a more sinister motive behind their play. Should she take away the dolls or the oven? Should she warn the parents to keep their 2-year-olds away from babies? Or should she bring in a mental health consultant?

Knowing that one of the children had a new sibling and another had one on the way, Aileen decided to involve the parents in talking through what the children might be thinking and feeling. The families' reactions varied from laughter to horror. However, each family had been very aware that it might face difficulties in bringing a new baby into the home. Together, they planned to broaden the children's information about babies. Soon the children were happily listening to stories about babies, feeding and bathing the baby dolls and rocking them to sleep, making pictures and mobiles for the new babies, asking lots of questions about what babies liked and what they could do, and boasting about their "big brother" and "big sister" skills. This play also became a safe place to "be angry with babies" when an older child in the play family felt left out. The oven play gradually diminished.

Aileen reflected on possible meanings of the children's play. She knew that reacting by firmly stopping the play risked making it more exciting, although she found it disturbing enough to want it to stop. Putting an end to the play also might be a missed opportunity to understand and explore its underlying meaning. She brought the parents together to share their observations and concerns. Then, she chose to respond to their play by supporting their interest in babies and providing a wider choice of themes to enrich their play. ✪

Illustration: Robert Saunders

- Use of rich language,

- Access to a variety of age appropriate materials,

- Methods of developmentally supportive guidance, and

- Cultural competence skills.

Informed, reflective infant care teachers. Infant care teachers should have a genuine love of babies. However, meeting each baby's rapidly changing needs also requires good observation skills and detailed understanding of child development. Training is essential.

Research on child care quality and its effects on children clearly links higher levels of education and specialized early childhood training with the provision of warmer, more responsive care, the use of more and varied language with young children, and better school readiness outcomes (Burchinal, Cryer, Clifford, & Howes, 2002). For children over age 3 years, having a teacher with a bachelor of arts degree may make such a difference to children's success in early grades that early childhood experts, advocates, and policymakers alike have urged that it be a requirement. For children under 3, most BA programs have very limited content devoted to infants and toddlers and their care in group settings. Notwithstanding this limitation, it is essential that infant and toddler care teachers have a strong working knowledge of infant and toddler development. For children under 2, the degree itself may be less important. It is essential, though, that infant and toddler care teachers have a strong working knowledge of infant–toddler development (Howes, Whitebook, & Phillips, 1992). This may be gained through college courses such as those required for a child development associate credential or for an associate of art degree or associate in science degree in early childhood education or through intensive training (such as that offered by Creative Curriculum, WestEd, and High/Scope [Dodge, Rudick, & Burke, 2006; Lally & Mangione, 1988–2007; Post & Hohmann, 2000]), accompanied by coaching and mentorship.

All teachers need ongoing opportunities to deepen their knowledge and talk about their practice with professional colleagues and mentors (Copa, Lucinski, Olsen, & Wollenburg, 1999). Caring for infants and toddlers is intimate on more than one level. The physical contact of touch in feeding, calming, diapering, and bathing creates an extraordinary ongoing intimate physical experience between people who are not related. Infant care teachers need support from the adult relationships available within the program to reflect on feelings such as "I have nothing left to give," "Nobody could help that baby stop crying all the time," or "How can such a young, helpless baby make me feel so angry?" Supportive adult relationships provide opportunities to experience, reflect on, and find a way to manage these difficult feelings.

Thoughtfulness and reflection regarding one's own reactions and decisions add to the infant care teacher's ability to really understand the children and respond appropriately to them. Several three-step approaches to reflective practice can be applied to the care and education of young children. Acknowledge, Ask, and Adapt (Program for Infant Toddler Caregivers, n.d.) or Respect, Reflect, Relate (Wittmer & Petersen, 2006) are both popular processes that ask the care teacher to observe the child, think about what the child's intentions are and what her own feelings are, consider possible reactions on her part, and choose a response that seems most useful.

A rich language environment sparks conversations (Bardige & Segal, 2004). Adults speak to children often about what they are doing. Intriguing objects and activities

Photo credit: Stephen Bobb

prompt children and adults to ask each other questions. Pictures of children's activities, family members, and favorite objects encourage labeling and stories. Pretend play materials and songs encourage word play, whereas quiet spaces with a few interesting objects foster intimate exchanges. Knowing that frequent reading with infants and toddlers boosts their language and cognitive development (Raikes et al., 2006), infant care teachers read with children several times a day and encourage parents to do the same.

Adults show genuine interest in what children think and feel by engaging them as conversation partners—even when the child's side of the conversation consists of coos, babbles, and gestures—or even, for young infants, just glances, movements, and smiles. Rather than formally instructing, good teachers offer comments, open-ended questions, and information that extend a child's idea and give the child time to respond. As teachers talk and play with individuals and small groups, they find many opportunities to support cognitive, social, and emotional development.

In a rich language environment, a young infant who cries upon waking can hear his trusted infant care teacher's voice saying, "I hear you, I'm coming!" Similarly, a mobile

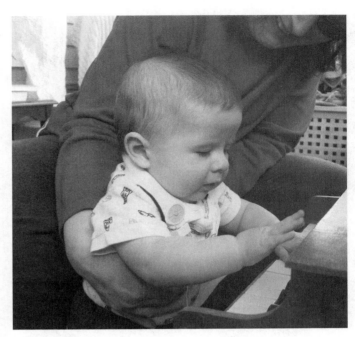

Photo credit: Kelly Rozwadowski

infant at the changing table may be verbally led through the routine in a comforting and soothing voice: "I am going to wipe your bottom with this wet wipe—it might be cold, get ready." Toddlers who are just beginning to talk need responsive infant care teachers ready to repeat

---

Kevin (7 months) was sitting on the floor tapping a soft rattle repeatedly on his lap; he was looking up at 5-year-old Nadine and smiling. Alvin (10 months) crawled over, took the rattle out of Kevin's hand, and crawled away. Kevin looked at Nadine, frowned, and burst into tears. Nadine quickly grabbed a rattle off of a nearby shelf and, with a big smile, shook it in front of Kevin's face. "Here Kevin, here's a rattle. It's okay. Don't cry." Kevin kept crying. Nadine shook the rattle harder, repeating, "You're okay. Here's a rattle." Kevin turned his head away from Nadine and cried louder.

Alea, their family child care teacher, quickly came to both children's rescue. Motioning to Nadine to join her, she sat next to Kevin on the floor. With a look of concern on her face, she said in a soft voice, "You're so sad." Then, pointing toward Alvin, "Alvin took your rattle again!" Kevin looked up at his infant care teacher but continued crying. She put her hand, and Nadine's, on Kevin's back and rubbed gently, saying, "Maybe Nadine and I can help you feel better." Kevin snuggled closer, whimpered for a bit, then took the rattle Nadine offered. "You really helped Kevin," Alea said to Nadine. "Thanks for being such a good friend."

Alea was pretty sure that Alvin had taken the rattle because it looked interesting, and not to make Kevin cry. Over the next few days, she made extra efforts to have duplicate toys available and to help Alvin and Kevin enjoy each others' company.

Acknowledging, asking, and adapting are the tools of responsive caregiving. Alea was able to acknowledge Kevin's feelings and Nadine's attempts to solve the problem. She reflected on the situation and decided that she could easily adapt the environment to accommodate two children with similar interests by making duplicate toys available. ✪

Photo credit: Kelly Rozwadowski

them. Later, the toddler may enjoy the same toys in pretend play.

The best toys are those that require the child to use his mind and body to make it work. Many toys on the market are battery operated and produce sounds and light when turned on. These may be briefly interesting to a baby but are limited in their usefulness and as a learning tool. They teach babies to be passive. Television and other materials that do not respond to the child's actions should not be part of an infant–toddler learning environment.

Infant–toddler teachers who create rich play and learning opportunities have high expectations for the children in their care. They see them as active, competent learners, and expect them to engage in challenging intellectual activities throughout the day. They create a world of wonder that babies can explore and master. During a typical play period, these teachers create numerous opportunities for children to be amazed, contemplative, and surprised (Lally, 2005).

Adults support learning by playing with individual children and small groups, following the children's lead. They continually design and adapt the space according to the current needs of the individual and the group. Adults set up opportunities that encourage children to play with each other, to move on their own, to make choices about materials, and to explore the world. Balls, mirrors, and toys to build with and cuddle, and that make noise when squeezed or shaken are all good for young infants. Mobile infants will enjoy containers to be filled and emptied, activity boxes, board books, and space to roll, crawl, and scoot. Young toddlers working at mastering walking enjoy push, pull, and riding toys. All babies enjoy playing with household materials such as spoons, measuring cups that stack, and pots and pans.

their words back to them and extend their language in a variety of ways. Toddlers whose home language is not English benefit when the teacher uses language along with a gesture or facial expression as it enhances his learning of the second language.

Age-appropriate materials. Infant–toddler care teachers should continually adapt the group space to meet the changing skills and interests of the children. Young infants spend much of their time being held, fed, diapered, and rested. However, over the first few months of life, they benefit from floor time on a comfortable carpet or stiff blanket. They enjoy mirrors and toys to look at, reach for, and mouth. They simply like being placed near each other on the floor and looking at each other. As the baby's abilities change, so should the materials available to them.

Toys should be chosen for how well they match and support the baby's current and emerging skills. The young infant enjoys looking at chunky cars, trucks, and animals. The same infant will soon enjoy reaching for them, mouthing them, shaking them, and throwing

In an inviting environment, babies find a variety of interesting objects, textures, and physical challenges arranged to encourage exploration without overwhelming them with too many choices (Curtis & Carter, 2003). Toys and furnishings need not be fancy or expensive, just safe, washable, engaging, and able to be used in different ways. Some toys should reflect the cultures represented in the program. Sufficient, well-chosen toys and sensory materials reduce conflicts and support imitation and cooperative play. However, it is the responsive voice of the infant care teacher that makes each play experience

William, the new director of the Wee Care center, was distressed when he observed the toddler room. The children seemed busy enough, and the room was bright, clean, and well stocked. However, the adults were spending so much time managing children and setting up activities that they were not engaging children in conversation. Recorded music substituted for singing and made it difficult to hear a toddler's early speech attempts. At story time, teachers seemed more intent on finishing the book or questioning children about the names and colors of pictured objects than on helping them talk about the story and connect it to their own experiences.

William decided to begin with books. He brought one of his favorites, *Pretend You're a Cat* (Marzollo & Pinkney, 1997), and read it to a few of the children. As he read, he asked the children to help him make the different animal sounds and act out their movements. Soon, the children were bringing over toy animals and eagerly talking about their pets and animals in their neighborhoods. To build upon the children's interest, William urged the teachers to gather leashes, feeding dishes, and other pet paraphernalia that the children could use for further play and conversation. He brought in some nature magazines so that the teachers could cut out animal pictures and help children paste them into their own "books." Over the next few months, William modeled various ways to get toddlers talking and arranged for the toddler teachers to meet once a week to talk about how to capitalize on the children's interests and enrich their conversations.

The opportunities for using language with infants and toddlers are endless. This director adapted the environment, adding materials to each play area that built upon the children's interests. He also brought the teachers together for professional development and the exchange of ideas. This way their interactions with the children supported the environmental changes and created a rich language environment. ✪

emotionally satisfying. The classroom should be designed with open spaces that invite free movement; barriers and soft (but firm) surfaces create areas for quiet play and conversation.

Developmentally appropriate guidance. Infant care teachers provide guidance as children learn to manage their own feelings and be members of a group. They help children regulate their emotions and behavior, gradually modifying their support as children mature. The teachers help children prepare for new experiences and transitions, and encourage self-control by setting clear, consistent limits and having realistic expectations. They help toddlers put strong feelings into words in order to resolve conflicts in positive ways. As a result, children hear many more *yeses* and words of deserved praise and encouragement than *nos*. It is also important to be aware and sensitive to the fact that cultural norms influence how families teach emotional regulation. Some cultures emphasize verbal interactions to help a child regulate his emotions, whereas other cultures emphasize physical proximity such as holding him when he is upset. Talking with families about their approach will be helpful in devising limit-setting strategies.

Within the group, infant care teachers help infants and toddlers learn about getting along with their peers. They help young infants to "touch gently." Mobile infants learn that there are rules about biting and pinching as teachers help children understand that the other child's experience is different from their own. Toddlers learn about ownership, sharing, and turn-taking. They learn that groups have rules about how meals are eaten, how laps are shared, and how tantrums are handled.

As the infant care teacher attends to the children's many urgent feelings and moments of conflict during the day, she may easily find herself fatigued and short of patience. Adults within a program need to continually offer each other support, perspective, and new ideas to assure that the infant care teachers are providing guidance and positive direction to the children. The director or supervisor can support the infant care teacher by bringing a new point of view to the situation.

Babies begin very early to learn which behaviors are acceptable and which are not by watching the reactions of their families and infant care teachers. A sharp "no" can be crushing to a toddler who counts on her infant

" I spend the whole day running interference," Susan complained to her supervisor. "As soon as I redirect one child, another one gets into trouble. I don't want to be saying no all of the time, but giving my toddlers other choices just isn't working."

"Toddlers can be trying," her supervisor sympathized, "and teaching them limits without putting a damper on their enthusiasm is always a challenge. Would you start by keeping a record of incidents? Maybe we can figure out together how to help the children learn to enjoy each other without hurting or getting hurt."

A few days later, Susan showed her supervisor her incident list. Two things were clear: First, most of the "troubles" involved one child grabbing a toy from another and the first child hitting to get it back. Second, these incidents were most likely to occur right before lunch, when the children were supposed to be cleaning up. When she observed Susan's classroom, the supervisor noticed something else: Susan intervened quickly when she saw trouble coming by redirecting the toddlers. She was trying so hard not to say no that she was missing opportunities to provide positive guidance and supply the language that could help the children control their behavior and teach them how to solve their conflicts without grabbing or hitting.

Together, Susan and her supervisor mapped out a course of action. At clean up time, Susan would ask each child to pick up a specific toy. She would put away some toys as well while staying close to the children who were most likely to grab toys. If she saw a child grabbing or hitting, she would say, "Let's tell Jeremy you want your truck back. Tell him, please give me my truck." This way she would protect the children while modeling an alternative, more prosocial approach. Finally, they would also adjust the schedule so that more of the cleanup happened when the children were less likely to be hungry.

Self-discipline is something we all work to accomplish throughout our lives. As is true for the development of other domains, children need manageable challenges, modeling of effective strategies, support and feedback, and opportunities to practice and achieve mastery. ✪

Photo credit: Kelly Rozwadowski

care teacher's affection. However, a lack of limits can also be frightening. When infant care teachers say "no" calmly but firmly, offer a simple explanation ("It hurts Cassie when you pull her hair"), give children words that help them control their behavior ("Touch gently") or handle a conflict ("Your turn now?"), and acknowledge and encourage children's good behavior ("You put your dolly away. Thanks for helping"), they build positive identity, social skill, self-reliance, and language ability (Hart & Risley, 1995).

Individually Appropriate Practice

Infants are unique beings, right from the beginning. They differ in abilities and interests. Parents and infant care teachers often notice these differences and notice that their personalities tend to persist over time. The infant–toddler care teachers provide individually appropriate care by the following:

• Meeting the needs of the individual within the group.

• Observing and planning.

Photo credit: Stephen Bobb

- Providing strength-based, inclusive care.

- Following a system for assessment, screening, and referral.

Meeting the needs of the individual within the group.
Infants are individuals. They differ from each other in many ways. Appreciating the uniqueness of each infant, observing him over time, learning his preferences and moods, and understanding his needs provide the infant care teacher with useful information. The care teacher is better able to understand and connect with the child and enrich the experience of group care for the child and family.

In an intimate setting, flexible scheduling is possible. Babies sleep when they want to sleep. They eat when they are hungry, and are offered foods that meet their individual needs. Infants and toddlers can play when they want to play with plenty of opportunities to explore a variety of toys and materials. Because babies' rhythms are individual, an infant care teacher can expect that, at any given time, one of her infants might be sleeping, whereas another is absorbed in quiet play while she is actively engaging a third. In providing an intimate setting, the infant care teacher recognizes mobile infants' and toddlers' need to explore, assert autonomy, and periodically reconnect with the secure base their teacher provides.

Infant care teachers observe differences in even the youngest babies in their care, describing babies as "quiet," "easy going," or "active." Researchers describe people's characteristic styles of reacting and responding as *temperament*. Infant care teachers will recognize three common temperament types, or characteristic styles of engaging the physical and social environment:

- A *flexible* child is generally open to new people and experiences, is not alarmed by sudden occurrences, and adapts quickly to what is going on.

- A *feisty* child is energetic, active, and has strong reactions.

- A *fearful* child may appear shy and easily alarmed, and take extra time approaching new people, activities, or objects.

Understanding children's temperaments helps infant care teachers provide responsive care to each individual. Any temperamental trait can be an asset or a liability. For example, a child we might describe as "slow to warm" in the United States may be seen as culturally normal in an Asian country. A supportive infant care teacher can, over time, help a feisty or fearful child handle potentially distressing situations. How parents and infant care teachers respond to the child's temperament can play a big role in the child's emotional development, as the feedback that the child gets from adults contributes to the child's developing self-image.

Temperamental differences are an important piece of the puzzle. Young children's behavioral patterns are also influenced by cultural and familial caregiving practices (Day & Parlakian, 2004), health and situational factors, and the child's ongoing experience. Developmental transitions create predictable challenges, which each child negotiates in his own way (Brazelton, 1992). Careful observation and documentation of children's activity patterns, developmental advances, and responses to everyday challenges can help parents, infant care teachers, and sometimes consultants work together to interpret behavior and provide optimal support for each child.

Observing and planning. Providing responsive care changes the character of "planning lessons." Responsive infant care teachers observe the children every day, keeping

Danisha, 28 months, came into the group clinging to her mom and saying, "No, no, no." Lupe, her primary infant care teacher, was surprised. Danisha was usually happy as sunshine in the morning. "We had a very bad night," her mother said. "Our neighbor's house was on fire. There were fire trucks and sirens and everyone was screaming. I should stay home with her today, but I can't miss work."

Lupe gently took Danisha from her mother and held and rocked her until she calmed. "I heard about the big fire last night," Lupe said. "You saw firemen and fire trucks. I have some fireman dolls and trucks in my closet. Would you like me to show them to you?" Danisha nodded and they went together to the toy closet. Danisha took all of the firemen and their trucks to the block area and spent much of the next several weeks saving houses from fires.

The infant care teacher followed Danisha's interest and adapted the environment with materials for Danisha to use in play. She let Danisha make the choice, being careful not to overwhelm her with images that might remind her of the fire. In this way, Danisha is setting her own curriculum. ✪

Illustration: Robert Saunders

notes and taking photographs when they can. Current approaches to curriculum planning encourage using this documentation of the children's play and emerging milestones to guide planning for materials and activities to bring to the group. In this way, the baby is really determining his own curriculum though his skills and interests, and the observant teacher is supporting the child's attempts to gather information about the world.

For example, one day as the mobile infants were in the play yard, Luis noticed a little beetle. He excitedly flapped his arms and smiled at the infant care teacher, Norma, showing her his treasure. Norma said, "Woo! A bug!" Luis said, "Buh, buh." "The bug is crawling, Luis," added Norma. "Here, look at this," as she handed him a large, unbreakable magnifying glass. "Buh, buh, buh," Luis said. Later that day, Norma chose a book with pictures of bugs to look at with Luis. The next morning she set a basket of toy rubber bugs in the block area. Norma used her observations of Luis to change her classroom materials to reflect his interests.

Infant care teachers sometimes find it difficult to record observations when they are already so busy meeting the needs of the babies in their care. Some successful strategies used by care teachers include using sticky notes to jot down observations and then sticking them into the child's file, carrying a clipboard with a sheet of paper for each child, or keeping a camera handy. Some care teachers take pictures of the children's art work or building projects to demonstrate their increasing skill over time.

A series of photos taken to document a child's interest or activities can be mounted on cardboard and posted on the wall for the children to look back on or placed in a small photo album for the children to thumb through. Families and infant care teachers can look at the pictures together to appreciate the child's point of view. Materials and activities can then be offered at home and at child care to support the child's understanding of the things that interest her.

Providing strength-based, inclusive care. Fortunately, child care of all kinds is becoming "inclusive" by opening its doors to infants and toddlers with special needs. The Americans With Disabilities Act requires public and private child care programs to accept children with special needs and to make reasonable accommodations to serve them.

Providing developmentally appropriate group care for infants and toddlers with special needs may involve specialized care during daily routines (Segal & Masi, 2001), availability of medically necessary devices, or use of assistive technology. When the group includes children who are receiving early intervention services or have special medical needs, these services are integrated into the ongoing activities of the group. Group care also offers opportunities to promote the healthy development of infants and toddlers with, or at risk of, emotional or behavioral disorders.

Infant care teachers have experience with the typical variations in development. They are to observe individual children closely over time and in a range of situations. The infant care teacher adapts her caregiving to the child with special needs in the same way she would meet the individual needs and interests of any other child. If necessary, she would also receive special training from the parents, a medical provider, or an early intervention specialist. These experts would be available for her to call upon for situations beyond her expertise. Some services, such as feeding through a gastrostomy tube or suctioning a tracheotomy, may come under the state's Nurse Practice Act. It would be against the law for a care teacher to provide the service. Infant care teachers and directors should clarify this before agreeing to provide specific services.

Often the biggest barrier to enrolling a child with a unique need is fear of the unknown. Many care teachers think that they need to be experts on a child's disability or syndrome in order to care for her safely and not make mistakes. In fact, their expertise in providing responsive care to infants and toddlers and their parents is likely to be far more important.

A system of observation, screening, referral, and follow-up. Infant care teachers systematically observe children, document progress, and address concerns. Children who are cared for on a regular basis receive routine screenings for hearing and vision, overall health, and development. Families, teachers, administrators, and specialists partner to keep up-to-date records, implement recommendations, and refer children for additional assessments or interventions when concerns arise.

Some center-based programs have professionals on staff who can track children's development on a regular basis

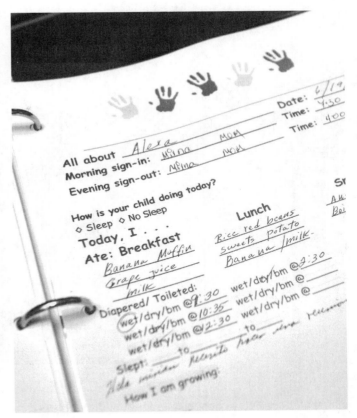

Photo credit: Stephen Bobb

Brian was born prematurely with a variety of medical and developmental issues. For the first 6 months, his mother was able to stay home with him. When she needed to return to work, she approached a neighbor who took care of her own granddaughter and another little girl. The neighbor knew and liked Brian and thought she would enjoy a baby, but she had one concern. It takes Brian 1 hour to finish a four-ounce bottle. How could she care for the other children if she was feeding Brian all of the time?

Inclusion of children with special needs can present real difficulties. The time Brian needed to eat would have made it impossible for the neighbor to provide care. However, a third neighbor, a retired school teacher who loved children, solved the problem by offering to be the home provider's emergency backup. She offered to come in twice a day to feed Brian. She was not paid, but over time Brian's family "adopted" her as a grandma, inviting her to family dinners and filling a void in her life. ☺

Photo credit: Stephen Bobb

permission. Family child care; centers with fewer on-site resources; and family, friend, and neighbor care can be supported by developmental specialists, infant–toddler specialists, or infant mental health specialists who are based in resource and referral organizations, early intervention programs, health care clinics, or other community agencies.

Infant mental health experts recommend that care teachers consider a referral for mental health services if the child's behavior:

- Has markedly changed or causes parents and other infant care teachers to consider the child "difficult";

- Makes satisfying interactions with others difficult;

- Is observed in multiple settings by multiple people; and

- Persists over time (Parlakian & Seibel, 2002).

and screen for delays or social–emotional difficulties if concerns arise. They also may have ongoing relationships with pediatricians or clinics and with early intervention providers who can provide education for their staff and also address the needs of individual children, with family

Infant care teachers and their supervisors play critical roles in identifying problems that warrant further investigation, supporting parents through the referral and diagnostic process, and working with families to implement recommendations and monitor their results.

At 2½, Angelina began to have difficulty with morning good-byes. She had been with her family child care provider, Sonia, since early infancy, and both she and her mother felt comfortable with Sonia and her home. Now, however, Angelina was crying every morning, clinging to her mom, and continuing to cry after her mom left. Fortunately, Sonia's home was part of a family child care system that provides consultants who visit each home on a monthly basis, mentor the provider, assess the children's development, and address parent and provider concerns.

Supported by her program consultant, Sonia worked with Angelina's mom to develop a new morning routine for Sonia and the much-loved stuffed bunny that she brought from home. For the first week, the routine worked like a charm; then the crying escalated.

With Angelina's parents' permission, the director brought in an early childhood mental health clinician. Her observations and her meetings with the family revealed that Angelina's mother was struggling with depression and feelings of inadequacy as a parent. Angelina was frequently anxious and tearful at home. The clinician suggested weekly play sessions with Angelina and her mother together, in addition to treatment for the mother's depression. Sonia continued to support and reassure Angelina's mother. Within a month, Angelina was showing markedly less anxiety and could settle happily into her day with Sonia.

Sensitive observation and a process for referral can lead to effective early intervention. ◗

Miguel's father confided to Oscar, the center director, that he was worried when he saw his 26-month-old son playing at cooking and housecleaning. It was not an appropriate role for men in his culture. Oscar promised to bring the issue up at staff meeting, and did so. Some staff saw a conflict between respecting cultural values and tolerating sexism. Oscar acknowledged the conflict, but wondered whether Miguel's father's concern might be less about what he saw as "feminine" play and more about the lack of opportunity for his son to explore "masculine" roles and develop a positive male identity.

This opened three areas of important discussion for the staff. First, many of the toddler care teachers were unsure how to handle it when boys wanted to "dress up" in ladies' hats and shoes and carry purses or when girls wore the men's suit jackets in the play area. Second, why were dramatic play themes limited to what goes on in a house? Third, were there props related to the children's culture, family, and communities that should be brought into the dramatic play area?

The discussion that followed revealed that some toddler care teachers shared Miguel's father's discomfort with crossing traditional gender lines, whereas others had fiercely held beliefs that these were forms of sexism. The conversation moved on to how the different families and cultures they served had different ideas about gender roles and how impossible it seemed to find solutions that would be suitable for all. In addition, many of the teachers wanted larger, more flexible, and more varied props for the children's dramatic play, whereas others felt that they were trying to push preschool play themes on toddlers who were just beginning to explore dramatic play.

The meeting became more reflective as the teachers came to appreciate how complex issues of caring for other's people's young children can be.

Because this team takes the time for reflection and discussion, the team members truly appreciate how difficult it can be to find solutions that may satisfy every parent and staff member when issues arise. The feelings, values, and beliefs that guide us as we care for infants and toddlers are deeply held. Varying life experiences and cultural backgrounds may imbue even the simplest event with great meaning. Sometimes, the first step to finding solutions is to appreciate the complexity of several people sharing responsibility for the well-being of young children. ⊕

Culturally and Linguistically Appropriate Practice

Each child's growing sense of identity is grounded in his or her own family's culture. In subtle, everyday routine interactions, infants and toddlers learn their culture's values, how people treat each other, and what is important and acceptable. If the child and the infant care teacher come from different cultures or speak different languages, it will take thoughtful planning to provide the child experiences and lessons that reflect her own culture. The child's sense of self evolves from her cultural and social contexts, including gender, race, ethnicity, social and economic class, family language, and family composition, along with her individual characteristics.

Photo credit: Stephen Bobb

The basic acts of caring—feeding, comforting, toileting, playing, and conversing—are shaped by the infant care teacher's values. Because these reflect her own childhood, professional training, and other cultural influences, self-awareness is the first step toward providing culturally sensitive care. Being aware of and reflecting on their own beliefs and values ensures that they do not interfere with the child's growth. Exploring their own backgrounds helps teachers become aware of the roots of their beliefs and practices. For example, an infant care teacher raised to feel that independence and early mastery of skills are important may see mealtimes as an opportunity to strengthen children's small motor skills by encouraging self-feeding. An infant care teacher who grew up in a culture where the availability of food was a concern may want to convey that food must never be wasted and exercise more control over how the baby eats. Training and supervision can help infant care teachers recognize their deeply rooted values and how they transmit them to the children (Day & Parlakian, 2004).

Reflecting on their backgrounds, beliefs, and reasons for choosing the work they do helps infant care teachers be honest with themselves and with families. A teacher must also be genuinely interested in the parent's beliefs, values, and point of view. Teachers must also be willing to examine their own beliefs, appreciate that there are multiple perspectives on child rearing, stay open

to a parent's point of view when there are differences, and be willing to change some of their practices (Day & Parlakian, 2004). Leaving room for flexibility ultimately sets the stage for resolving conflicts.

Infant care teachers who use a baby's home language reinforce his sense of belonging in both the home and the child care environment. Welcoming a child's family members into the child care setting and respecting their child-rearing values and beliefs, as well as their language and traditions, help a baby build a positive early identity. To provide cultural continuity, infant care teachers who do not share a child's language and culture can enlist colleagues, parents, or community members to provide linguistic and cultural mediation and help them build relationships with children and their families.

Many infants and toddlers have the opportunity to learn more than one language through everyday experiences at home, in child care, and in the community. Learning two languages simultaneously does not create language confusion; on the contrary, it enhances cognitive ability and flexibility (Petitto & Dunbar, in press). When an infant care teacher does not speak a child's home language, she can learn how to offer him affection, reassurance, and encouragement in his home language while also supporting

Photo credit: Stephen Bobb

his acquisition of her language (Genishi, 2002). A few endearing words in their home language can help a baby and his family feel more comfortable and secure in a child care setting where their language is not the dominant one. At the same time, infant care teachers who do a lot of talking with babies in a language (or languages) in which they are fluent themselves can provide good support for language learning by building upon the child's emerging language skills. For example, a bilingual infant care teacher whose primary language is Spanish may make a point of always speaking English to an Hispanic dual-language learner. However, she would better support his language learning by providing continuity with his home experience and using the fluency of her own richer, primary language.

Program Structures That Support Relationships

Ideally, in group care, the care teacher develops responsive, meaningful relationships with each child and supports their relationships with each other. However, being responsive to several babies at once can be challenging. Programs can be organized in ways that specifically support the development and maintenance of relationships or, conversely, in ways that make it difficult for even the best teachers to achieve meaningful relationships with the children and their families. Infant care teachers may not have the authority to make these decisions, but program directors and owners should consider how their program structures support the development of relationships. Relationships can develop when group care has

- Low child-to-teacher ratios and small groups,
- Primary caregiving,
- Continuity of care,
- Responsive routines, and
- An engaging environment.

Low ratios (few children per infant care teacher) and small groups provide opportunities for babies and infant care teachers to get to know each other well. Primary caregiving—the assignment of one infant care teacher to a few children—helps teachers get to know the children and their families well and establishes a clear pathway of communication. Continuity of care means having one primary infant care teacher for over 1 year, preferably for the first 3 years of life. Responsive routines provide a structure for one-on-one interactions within the group. An engaging environment keeps babies interested and active without the constant involvement of an adult.

Low Ratios and Small Group Sizes

In child care research studies, low child-to-staff ratios and small group sizes are consistently correlated with more frequent, more playful, and warmer interactions between adults and children, more positive interactions among children, better overall environments for learning, and better outcomes for children (NICHD & ECCRN, 1996). The number should be small enough to ensure safety, close relationships with adults, and a level of noise, activity, and social stimulation that each child can handle.

How small of a group is small enough for good-quality infant–toddler child care depends upon a number of factors:

- The size and configuration of the space,
- The training and skill of the infant care teachers,
- The amount and type of stimulation and adult attention that is optimal for each child, and
- The availability of help in an emergency.

The American Academy of Pediatrics recommends the following group sizes and ratios for infants and toddlers in centers and in large family child care homes (American Academy of Pediatrics, 2002).

Age	Maximum child-to-staff ratio	Maximum group size
Birth–12 months	3:1	6
13–30 months	4:1	8
31–35 months	5:1	10

Note. Reprinted with permission.

Abby, an experienced infant care teacher, was thrilled with the new policy of three infants per primary infant care teacher. Now, finally, she felt that she could take the time to really know her charges and support their learning. Mealtimes, especially, were relaxed and pleasant. Typically, she would feed Simon his bottle while sitting on the floor with Tule and Martin, sing Simon to sleep, and then feed Tule and Martin in their highchairs.

While chatting with Tule and Martin about their rice and vegetables one day, she sprinkled a few oat "O"s on Tule's tray. Tule leaned forward in her chair and struggled to grasp an "O" between her index finger and thumb. Abby noticed that she seemed to have a hard time "aiming" at just one "O," so she spread out the cluster to make the task a bit easier. Tule watched this, studied this new landscape for a moment, then reached for and latched onto an "O." "You got one, Tule!" Abby exclaimed as Tule attempted to deposit the "O" in her open mouth. Although she could grasp, Tule had not quite mastered the necessary and critically important release component of this task. As her mouth closed, the "O" dropped into her lap. "Here it is, Tule," said Abby. Slowly, so that Tule could watch, she reached to retrieve the "O" and put it back on the tray. "And here are more carrots for you, Martin," she said smiling at him.

Time after time Tule tried to grasp and eat an "O." A few even found their way into her mouth. Abby looked for opportune moments when Tule would accept a spoonful of cereal or pureed peas into her mouth, and periodically replenished the tray with three or four more "O"s. Sometimes she put the "O"s close together, other times she spread them to the corners of the tray. Whenever Tule looked toward her, Abby would comment, "You're getting them," or "You got it!" Martin, meanwhile, had grabbed the spoon, smeared his right cheek with carrots, and was looking at Abby while vigorously banging the spoon on his tray. With each "bang," he squinted at Abby. "Bang!" Abby said, as she squinted back. As she offered him a bite with a new spoon, he grinned, delighted with the game.

Illustration: Robert Saunders

Small groups create a sense of intimacy and safety. Rich dialogue between infant care teachers and babies is possible in small groups because there are fewer bodies, less noise, and less activity. There is time to learn the more subtle cues of infants and toddlers with chronic illnesses or disabilities. With low child-to-staff ratios and small groups, infant care teachers can build strong relationships with individual children and adapt activities and arrange furniture and equipment to meet the changing interests and capacities of the group. It is also easier to get to know the children's families. When adults can talk comfortably in a quiet place, they can begin to build trusting relationships and appreciate cultural and linguistic differences. ⊗

The American Academy of Pediatrics recommendations are more stringent than those required for National Association for the Education of Young Children (NAEYC) accreditation. NAEYC recommends maximum child-to-staff ratios of 3:1 or 4:1 (with maximum group sizes of 6 and 8) for infants up to 15 months, 3:1 or 4:1 (with group sizes up to 12) for toddlers 12–28 months, and 4:1, 5:1, or 6:1 (with group sizes up to 12) for toddlers 21–36 months.

In home settings where one provider cares for up to six children by herself, the academy recommends no more than four children if one of them is under 2 years old, and only two children if both of them are under 2. Early Head Start requires a ratio no higher than four infants or toddlers per care teacher and group sizes no larger than eight children.

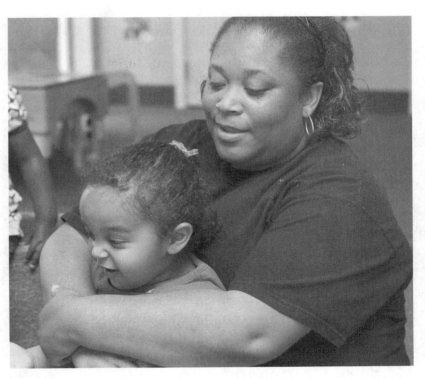

Photo credit: Stephen Bobb

Kallie had several different infant care teachers before joining Hanna's group at 12 months. She was wary of this strange new adult. Aisha, Kallie's mother, used many temporary caregivers and expected Kallie to settle with strangers quickly. Hanna's program valued primary caregiving and close relationships. Hanna asked Aisha to help her incorporate familiar comforts into Kallie's day at the center: words, music, a special blanket, family pictures, routines, and anything else that would help establish continuity between Kallie's home and center lives. Knowing that Kallie would feel safer if she saw that her mother trusted Hanna and was comfortable at the center, Hanna encouraged Aisha to bring Hanna for several visits before leaving her and to call or drop in at any time.

Hanna had established close, long-standing relationships with her other two toddlers and their families. In the mornings and evenings, the adults chatted and played with the children like friends getting together. Hanna encouraged Aisha to spend time at the center. With a little encouragement, Aisha became comfortable with the other families. In her first few days in Hanna's group, Kallie learned the name of one of the toddlers—Emma—who had been with Hanna since she was 6 months old. Kallie and Emma's interest in each other was reassuring to Hanna. Aisha was becoming more aware that relationships mattered to her daughter. They talked about ways to use this blossoming friendship to help Kallie feel safe and comfortable. Emma's trust and love of Hanna seemed to help Kallie want to be close to Hannah as well. Before long, Kallie was thriving, and the friendship between Kallie and Emma had extended to their respective families.

Primary caregiving gives each child and his family someone special with whom to build a relationship. The role of the primary infant care teacher is to build a relationship between herself, the child, and the parent—and to strengthen the parent–child relationship. The better the infant care teacher knows the family, the easier it will be for her to get to know the child. The better an infant care teacher knows a child, the more easily she can understand the child's communications and provide both comfort and appropriate challenge. Similarly, the better a child knows his infant care teacher, the more he can anticipate her response to his actions. ☺

Photo credit: Stephen Bobb

Primary Caregiving

Low ratios and small group sizes are only part of the answer. When each baby is assigned to one care teacher as a primary caregiver, the teachers are able to form deep, enduring relationships with babies. That teacher partners with the child's family and facilitates the child's relationships with the other children and adults in the setting. Two infant care teachers may work as a team, with each taking primary responsibility for certain children and using the other as back-up when necessary. Decisions about grouping, staffing, transitions, and scheduling are made with sensitivity to each child's needs for stable, growing relationships with adults and peers.

Continuity of Care

Getting to know another person takes time. Systems that implement continuity of care ensure adequate time for teachers, children, and families to get to know each other by keeping a group of children and their teacher together for at least 1 year (ideally 2 or 3 years, however). This system also minimizes abrupt transitions that disrupt relationships and that can be very difficult for babies. When a very young child changes infant care teachers, he may mourn the loss and feel sad and angry. Without his trusted guide, he may be unsure of how to act and hesitant to explore. Too many changes can create a reluctance

to form new relationships (Lally, Torres, & Phelps, 1993). Parents and care teachers may also suffer when children have frequent changes in groups or teachers. They too may have a difficult time building a trusting relationship with a new person.

Continuity of care is one of the inherent benefits of family child care. Children are likely to remain in the same setting and with the same adult(s) for 3 to 5 years and may come back for after-school care during their elementary school years. Child care centers are more likely to move children to new groups with new teachers on a yearly basis. Some move children to new classrooms throughout the year, in order to maintain full enrollment or to comply with mandated or recommended group sizes and staff-to-child ratios.

If young children routinely move up to a different classroom when they reach a certain age, their distress can affect both the friends they leave behind and the members of their new group. Infants and toddlers miss their friends and the play routines they have developed together. In the new classroom, a group of toddlers who have been together for a while may have difficulty sharing their teacher, toys, and friends with a newcomer. A child with a new teacher who does not yet know her signals and needs has to work harder to get her thoughts and feelings across. When the child is frustrated in her efforts to communicate, she may act out her frustration in ways that create conflict.

Continuity builds relationships among teachers and parents as well as among children. Solid long-term relationships are especially important when a child's special needs require intense collaboration between parents and the toddler care teacher or when language or cultural differences need time to bridge.

Responsive Routines

Much of a young child's day in group care consists of routines such as greetings and departures, feeding, diapering and toileting, and sleeping. These routines provide opportunities to concentrate on an individual child and on peer relationships within the group. For infants and toddlers, each child's routine care should be based on his own readiness for feeding, diapering and toilet learning, and sleep.

Greetings and departures. Each child and parent should be greeted personally and warmly by the infant care teacher on arrival at the home or center and sent off at the end of the day with a smile and pleasant wishes. Arrivals and departures are times when families and care teachers can exchange information about the child's day or night, new interests, and health concerns. Some of the best moments are when a care teacher is able to express to the parent how much she likes and enjoys the baby. When care teachers have time to share a story about something funny or endearing the child did during the day, they are also letting the parent know how much they appreciate their wonderful child.

Greetings and departures are times that care teachers build their own relationship with each family member. Using the family member's name, asking about their well-being, and following up on previous conversations all help family members feel welcome, important, and valued within the child care program.

Feeding. Babies are fed their bottles in their care teacher's arms when they are hungry and not on a predetermined schedule. When children begin to feed themselves, snack and meal times become social events, with two or three older infants or toddlers eating finger foods or wielding spoons at a small table together. Care teachers talk with babies and toddlers during mealtimes and encourage interaction among the children.

Feeding routines are rooted in and highly influenced by cultural values and expectations. Some cultures believe that children should be demonstrating autonomy by eating independently by 1 year; others feel that food is a precious commodity and children should be carefully fed to avoid any waste. Perspectives about independence versus interdependence vary widely across cultures. Some programs emphasize the cooperative nature of mealtimes by serving from communal serving dishes, whereas others have children bring meals from home and prohibit any sharing.

Many factors can influence what foods a child may eat. These include allergies such as being lactose intolerant, cultural preferences or religious restrictions, or family choices such as being vegetarian. Care teachers must talk

---

Meeting the Continuity of Care Challenge

There is no one-size-fits-all way to provide continuity of care. Effective models include the following:

- *Multiage groups*, common in family child care but increasingly found in centers, enable younger children to learn from older ones and older children to nurture younger ones.

- *Looping* keeps a primary infant or toddler care teacher with a same-age group for 2 or 3 years. The group may expand to include new children. Smaller infant groups may combine into a larger toddler group. They may move as a group to a new, larger space as they grow. When her toddlers move on to preschool, the toddler care teacher picks up a new group of infants.

- *Stable, year-long, or 18-month-long assignments* of primary infant care teachers enable children to move up as a group to a toddler room with new teachers. The groups get to know their new teachers and surroundings during a planned transition period.

---

with families to understand what foods may or may not be served to their child.

Infant–toddler programs should encourage the feeding of breast milk. Breast milk has the right combination of fat, sugar, water, and protein for a baby's growth and development. It provides some protection from bacteria and viruses. Breast milk may provide long-term benefits such as lower likelihood of obesity and other diseases and some cognitive advantages (Women's Health.gov, 2005). A quiet, private space should be available for any parents where they can breast- or bottle-feed their baby. Programs should have the capacity to safely store and handle breast milk.

Diapering and toilet learning. Teachers should change diapers promptly and check diapers regularly (Gorski, 1999). Procedures for diapering should be sanitary and limit the spread of disease. Infant care teachers should use diapering as an opportunity for a pleasant, quiet moment with a child. The care teacher can describe

Photo credit: Stephen Bobb

what she is doing, using language that shows affection and concern for the child's well-being (e.g., "There, that's going to feel better. I like to keep you dry and comfortable")

Families may express concerns about male care teachers changing diapers. These concerns should be heard respectfully and sensitively resolved.

The timing and process of toilet learning is another area of routine care that varies widely in different cultures, and families and care teachers may bring different expectations to this task. Infant care teachers need to plan with families how they will go about toilet training so that their approaches are mutually supportive and not confusing to the child. Information to consider includes the following:

- How do you recognize the child is developmentally ready?

- How is the child expressing interest in toilet learning?

- What method is the family using at home?

- How does the family or program feel about the balance between privacy needs and toileting with peers? Do gender differences matter to the family or program in the sharing of bathroom space?

Sleep. Infants and toddlers are likely to need one or more naps during the day. Again, teachers and families should share information on how the baby is used to going to sleep or what the toddler's nap routines are. Is the baby rocked to sleep or placed on her back in the crib to fall asleep alone? Is there a lullaby she hears as she falls asleep?

The American Academy of Pediatrics suggests these practices to limit the risk of sudden infant death syndrome (SIDS):

1. Always place babies on their backs to sleep, even for short naps.

2. Place babies in a safety-approved crib with a firm mattress (cradles and bassinets may be used, but choose those that are certified for safety by the Juvenile Products Manufacturers Association; www.jpma.org).

3. Remove soft, fluffy bedding and stuffed toys from the baby's sleep area.

4. Make sure the baby's head and face remain uncovered during sleep.

5. Place the baby in a smoke-free environment.

6. Allow the baby to sleep in light clothing to avoid overheating. If a blanket is used, make sure the baby's feet are at the bottom of the crib, that the blanket comes up no higher than the baby's chest, and that it is tucked in on the bottom and two sides of the crib. Consider using a sleep sack or a wearable blanket instead.

7. If you are working in a family child care home or center, create a written safe sleep policy to ensure that staff and families understand and practice back-to-sleep and SIDS risk reduction practices in child care. If you are a parent with a child in out-of-home child care, advocate for the creation of a safe sleep policy (Healthy Childcare America, nd).

Engaging Environments

Well-designed environments for infants and toddlers promote relationships, provide visual and physical information about pathways and boundaries, and offer opportunities for young children to explore. In many ways, the space becomes a strong element of the curriculum for infants and toddlers who spend so much time exploring, using their bodies, and watching each other from safe places.

Engaging environments feel like home (Modigliani & Moore, 2005). Indoor and outdoor spaces are clean, welcoming, and aesthetically pleasing. Full-sized furniture invites adults to hold and cuddle young infants, whereas private spaces for breast- or bottle-feeding encourage parents to come in and feed their baby during the day. Convenient storage makes routines efficient, keeping infant care teachers available to children. Low barriers between spaces maintain visible and audible access to every part of the room for an infant care teacher who may be diapering, feeding, or rocking a baby.

Ample space allows children to interact with others or play alone, actively, or quietly. Fifty square feet of usable play space (not counting cabinets, counters, diapering areas, and cribs) is the per-child minimum for quality, although it far exceeds the usual 35 square feet required in most licensing regulations. Mixed-age groups need even more space to accommodate a wider range of activities and safety needs (White & Stoecklin, 2003).

Photo credit: Stephen Bobb

Illustration: Robert Saunders

The director of an infant–toddler child care program was reminded of the importance of sharing the caring when she cared for her 2½-year-old granddaughter while her parents were away. "One very early morning, my granddaughter asked again where her mother was. I explained about her mommy and daddy's vacation and that I would be there to take care of her in their absence and would stay until they returned. 'Oh,' she said, 'then you'll be the mommy.' I remember saying, 'Yes but,' attempting to explain how I would be caring for her. At the same time I was very much in touch with my discomfort about 'being the mommy.' I could do the mommy things in her parent's absence—the feeding, bathing, hugging, reading stories, playing together, and getting ready for bed—but I wouldn't be the mommy."

She goes on to explain, "My granddaughter taught me that in the absence of the mommy, somebody must take the mommy's place, to do the things that mommies and daddies do in order for the toddler to continue to feel loved and secure. 'Holding the place' for the parent to return to the toddler is the role of the teacher in the child care setting. She is at her absolute best when she is second best, providing the secure base in the absence of the parent that allows the child to continue to move forward."

Photo credit: Stephen Bobb

The environment should provide opportunities for the infant or toddler to pursue his current interests. For example, most toddlers are interested in climbing. If a program provides a climbing ladder bolted to the wall, a few stairs leading to a raised platform, and a ramp that provides a window view of the play yard or the next room; the toddler's natural interest in climbing will be safely satisfied. However, if no equipment is available for climbing, the toddler is likely to improvise, using shelves, tables, and even friends as tools for climbing. When this activity is met with reprimands, the child learns that his interests are not "right" and his curiosity and exploration may be dampened (Torelli & Durrett, nd).

An indoor space must meet the many needs of infants and toddlers, their care teachers, and their families. In addition to large and open spaces, young children need spaces that feel private to them where they can look at books, play, or take a break even while enabling the teacher to still observe them. This is especially important for shy children for whom being in a group all day can be stressful, raising their level of cortisol. Cortisol is a hormone released into the brain when a person is stressed. It sends a "flight or fight" message and, in larger quantities, destroys brain cells (Watamura, Donzella, Alwin, & Gunnar, 2003). The stress of being in a noisy, active group all

day long may contribute to the aggression and tears all too often seen in toddler programs.

It takes a great deal of planning—and frequent rearrangement—to create spaces that work for children, care teachers, and families. An environment that is soothing for infants and convenient for their care teachers may need to be enlarged and subdivided when the babies become mobile, providing destinations for crawlers and safe areas for quiet activity. Flooring, lighting, ceiling-hung canopies, platforms (5 inches), low walls, and low, secure shelving can all define spaces for infants and toddlers without restricting their visibility to care teachers. The long, straight path that allows proud new walkers to push toys all the way across the room may need to be modified when it becomes a raceway for exuberant toddlers.

Sometimes simple changes can make a big difference. The most basic principles of infant–toddler environmental design are also the most powerful:

• Create barriers to keep active children from intruding on those engaged in quiet pursuits;

• Create clear pathways for children and adults to move about;

• Make the environment flexible to accommodate the rapid changes in children's abilities;

• Organize materials in areas that invite children to use them appropriately; and

• Make it convenient for adults to supervise and carry out daily management tasks.

Family and Community Partnerships

Care teachers work to develop a sensitive, trusting, and respectful sharing-the-caring relationship with parents. Care teachers foster friendships, information sharing, and mutual support among the families they serve. Parents and staff may collaborate in program design, implementation, and evaluation.

Just as a care teacher may be "at her absolute best when she is second best," a center or family child care home is at its absolute best when it is the hub of a mutually supportive community of families and teachers. Care teachers and parents, as well as other family and community members, work as a team to promote the learning and well-being of the children. Each child's primary care teacher and parents keep each other informed of the child's daily activities, interests, and developmental leaps, and work together to understand new behavior and address challenges, in addition to working toward mutual cultural understanding. Family participation may go well beyond the family's own child. Parents and care teachers may work together to plan family events and to shape program improvements and policies. Parents may be involved in hiring new staff. Over time, families form friendships and become resources for each other.

The infant–toddler field has been increasingly aware of the power of cultural beliefs to evoke strong feelings around caring for infants and toddlers. These differences can result in conflicts so that training in cultural reciprocity serves infant–toddler care teachers and home providers very well. ZERO TO THREE's *Preventing Child Abuse and Neglect* (Seibel, Britt, Gillespie, & Parlakian, 2006) curriculum defines cultural reciprocity as a "two-way process of information sharing and understanding initiated by the service provider" (p. 5–6). The four steps of cultural reciprocity are as follows:

1. Learning about our own culture.

2. Learning about another person's culture.

3. Explaining the basis of our recommendations to others.

4. Collaborating with families to resolve any culturally based differences.

As in Early Head Start, in which family involvement is mandated, excellent centers and family child care homes forge partnerships with parents. They make supporting, educating, and empowering families central features of their program (Pope & Seiderman, 2000). For example, a parent who is invited to attend a family event or just "hang out" in the classroom may become a regular visitor, a volunteer, or perhaps join a parent committee. Eventually, that parent may be invited to join a policy-making board. Other parents may choose different levels and types of involvement such as attending parent–child and

---

Family Support America's Principles of Family Support Practice

1. Staff and families *work together* in relationships based on *equality* and *respect*.

2. Staff *enhance* families' *capacity to support* the growth and development of all family members—adults, youths, and children.

3. Families are *resources* to their own members, to other families, to programs, and to communities.

4. Programs *affirm* and *strengthen* families' cultural, racial, and linguistic *identities* and *enhance* their ability to function in a multicultural society.

5. Programs are *embedded* in their communities and contribute to a *community-building* process.

6. Programs advocate with families for services and systems that are *fair*, *responsive*, and *accountable* to the families served.

7. Practitioners work with families to *mobilize* formal and informal resources to support family development.

8. Programs are *flexible* and continually *responsive* to emerging family and community issues.

9. Principles of family support are *modeled* in all program activities, including planning, governance, and administration (Family Support America, 2001).

---

parent education events, contributing suggestions, sharing information, helping other families in times of need, or helping with program evaluation. An open-door policy says to parents—you are always welcome.

Responsible Financial and Program Management

Leadership is crucial to the success of most group efforts. Child care is most likely to be of high quality when program managers have a deep understanding of what infants, toddlers, and their families need to flourish

Photo credit: Stephen Bobb

or she needs, thinks, and feels" (Program for Infant Toddler Care, 2007). It describes the importance of planning based on building strong relationships and supporting child-directed learning. The importance of supporting cultural and family identity is also made clear. The philosophy then describes the role of the environment and six program policies that anchor their work: (a) primary care, (b) small groups, (c) continuity, (d) individualized care, (e) cultural responsiveness, and (f) inclusion of children with special needs.

It is the role of management to ensure that decisions made about the program organization, the assignment of care teachers, and the way in which local and state licensing regulations are met or exceeded are all consistent with the program's overarching philosophy of care.

and the role group care can play in supporting them. Leadership includes establishing a philosophy of care that guides the decisions made about the program. This includes beliefs about and understanding of how children learn and what they need from adults. It also includes the value placed on the qualities of the relationship between families and care teachers, and between management and staff, as well as among staff that make it possible for the care teacher to feel fully supported in her work. The program leadership also needs skills and knowledge in managing finances, meeting state and local licensing requirements, and running a business.

In its statement of philosophy of care, the Program for Infant Toddler Care states the following:

> Good infant care is neither baby-sitting nor preschool.
>
> It is a special kind of care that resembles no other.
>
> —*Program for Infant Toddler Care, 2007*

The statement goes on to articulate elements of a relationship-based program emphasizing the importance of preparing care teachers to "get 'in tune' with each infant they serve and learn from the individual infant what he

Reflective Supervision

The intimacy of working with infants, toddlers, and families can be very intense and at times overwhelming. The pressures of immediate needs for feeding, diapering, and comforting babies combined with the stresses experienced and shared by families are compounded by the low wages and sometimes difficult working conditions, creating a variety of pressures for the care teacher.

Some infant–toddler child care programs use a process called *reflective supervision* to help care teachers manage their own feelings and be more responsive to infants and families. Reflective supervision is the practice of meeting regularly with staff members to discuss their experiences, thoughts, and feelings related to the work. This supervision is characterized by three key components: (a) reflection (or thinking out loud), (b) collaboration, and (c) regular meetings. Using this approach, the role of the supervisor is to help the supervisee answer his or her own questions by

- Providing support and knowledge to guide decision making;

- Offering empathy to help supervisees explore their own reactions to the work; and

- Helping staff manage the stress and intensity of work with families (ZERO TO THREE Center for Program Excellence, 2002).

Reflective supervision can also help staff develop coping mechanisms to manage the often complex and intense feelings that arise while working with very young children. Providing staff an outlet to acknowledge the challenges, concerns, and ambivalence they encounter on the job is a crucial first step in preventing frustration and burnout. Furthermore, supportive interactions help staff develop the skills they need to respond effectively to the challenges of their work.

For example, in one program, a young infant was consistently brought to the center in a T-shirt and diaper in the middle of winter. Along with feeling concern for the child, the teacher was very angry with the parent. The director shared great concern for the child's well-being, but she also knew that this was a single mother with a mental illness. She wanted the program to support this mother in improving her ability to care for her child. Regular sessions of reflective supervision helped the care teacher acknowledge and explore her anger and then problem solve with the director how she might create a stronger alliance with the mother. By building a sense of partnership with this parent, the care teacher was able to help the mother see the child's need for using warm clothing even if he was only outside between the car and the center.

Some child care centers, family child care homes, and family, friend, and neighbor care providers may set up formal associations, systems, or even get-togethers in order to provide this support on a regular basis. Having someone to talk to who understands the intimacy and the pressure of the work can be very helpful in maintaining the care teacher and family alliance.

Effective Program Management

Quality is difficult to maintain given the economics of child care. Young families, often with limited incomes, find it difficult to pay for the real cost of care. Salaries are low and benefits are inconsistent for the child care workforce. However, programs with strong policies and procedures, budgeting, record keeping, and general administration can contribute to an effective, efficient program and a supportive environment with clear expectations for staff and families.

Effective program management is essential for quality care. This includes systems and policies that assure financial viability, ethical operation, compliance with regulatory requirements, recruitment and retention of qualified staff, and clear expectations of parents. Among family, friend, and neighbor infant care teachers, those who charge for their services and have formal agreements with families tend to provide higher quality care (Porter, Rice, & Rivera, 2006). Family child care providers benefit from training in running a small business, as well as in caring for young children in groups. In many states, center directors and multisite program administrators earn credentials that reflect training in management and supportive supervision as well as expertise in child development.

Written guidelines and competent administrators are just the beginning. A well-functioning program embodies respectful, responsive relationships. Parents and staff understand and support the program's philosophy and mission, and are actively involved in shaping its policies and planning for its future.

Ongoing Self-Evaluation and Research-Informed Practice

At the program level, maintaining state-of-the-art quality means that staff are engaged in ongoing learning. Quality

Photo credit: Realistic Reflections/Getty Images

Aparna and Sameer began their child care search when they were expecting their first child. They hoped to find a warm, homey place where they felt comfortable, with a knowledgeable care teacher who shared their values and could speak their home language.

They had interviewed several care teachers in their neighborhood and liked two of them, but they were concerned about stability. Would their child be able to stay with the same person for several years? What would happen if the care teacher was ill, or if her family needed her, or if she had to take on too many children to make ends meet? When they visited Tan's large family child care home, their fears were allayed. Tan was a licensed and accredited provider with many years of experience. Her home felt like just the kind of place they would want for their child. During their interview, Tan handed them a small book explaining her policies. It began with a statement of her philosophy, and included sections on fees, days and hours of operation, health and illness policies, accommodation of special needs, the provider and her assistants' qualifications, parent responsibilities, and an enrollment contract. Aparna and Sameer looked at each other. Their decision was made. They happily gave Tan a deposit to hold a place for their child in 6 months.

Clearly written policies allow families to enter into a contract with a program knowing that they have a full understanding of the program's expectations and responsibilities. Tan had clearly communicated expectations of the families that allowed her to run her child care business efficiently and reliably. ⊘

is a moving target: As new ideas and strategies are tested and new research becomes available, definitions of quality and instruments to measure it are revised. Health and safety practices—such as emergency procedures, immunization schedules, and feeding recommendations—are also constantly evolving as a result of work by organizations such as the National Safety Council and the American Academy of Pediatrics.

Although the basic principles of quality apply to all children and all settings, their successful application requires sensitivity to the strengths and needs of particular children, families, and teachers, and to the values of their communities and cultures. An established curriculum or approach developed by a commercial company may or may not be right for a particular setting, it may not be a good match with children's and teachers' home cultures, or its success may be tied to extensive staff training and parent support.

Continuous quality improvement involves assessing needs, setting goals, experimenting with new ideas, observing and documenting their implementation and impact, making collective judgments, and beginning the cycle again. Families are asked about their satisfaction and suggestions for improvement.

Taking excellent care of infants and toddlers in groups involves both art and science. Supervisors keep abreast of research by regularly accessing resources such as those listed at the end of chapter 3 of this volume, and seek to implement evidence-based practices (Center for Evidence-Based Practice, nd) that have been shown in numerous studies to produce the outcomes these supervisors seek for the children they serve. Supervisors realize that a single study is not definitive, and often consider each new finding in light of what they already know. A supervisor makes a point of sharing interesting discoveries and new ideas with colleagues and parents so that they can consider implications for practice together.

A System That Sustains Quality

It is easy to think of infant–toddler child care as the room in which you teach, the program where you work, or the family child care home you own. However, every group of infants and toddlers and their care teacher is influenced in some way by a much larger system. Elements of this system range from federal policies and funding opportunities to local training or referral services.

The federal government has dedicated funds to support families seeking care who have low incomes, who are on public assistance, or who are transitioning from public assistance to work. These funds, available through the Child Care Development Fund (CCDF), may be used to subsidize or pay for children's attendance in child care. A small percentage of these funds is used by states to support state-level initiatives to increase quality in infant–toddler care. States use CCDF infant–toddler funds to offer training, to support local Child Care Resource and Referral agencies that may offer classes or on-site technical assistance, or to develop networks of infant–toddler specialists who support individual programs.

Many states have created voluntary program standards that describe how care teachers and programs can best serve infants and toddlers. About half of the states have written Early Learning Guidelines for Infants and Toddlers that describe what infants and toddlers should be learning and doing. These standards or guidelines are almost always voluntary but may be incorporated into Quality Rating Systems of reimbursement that reward their use.

Individual programs may pursue national accreditation of their quality. The two major national professional organizations, the National Association for the Education of Young Children and the National Association of Family Childcare, each offer accreditation to their members. This process includes an application, an intensive self-study aligned with established standards, and an on-site evaluation of quality.

Getting involved in policy is another way individuals concerned with issues related to the well-being of very young

Photo credit: Stephen Bobb

children can become advocates for this vulnerable group. The Policy Center at ZERO TO THREE provides electronic newsletters on current issues that suggest actions that might be considered a "big voice for little children." The Policy Center is available through the ZERO TO THREE Web site (www.zerotothree.org).

Information about these resources and the extensive system of research and policies that guides the field of infant–toddler group care is available on each state's child care office Web site and on other Web sites listed in the resource section at the end of chapter 3.

References

American Academy of Pediatrics, American Public Health Association, Health Resources and Services Administration, Maternal and Child Health Bureau. (2002). *Caring for our children. National health and safety performance standards: Guidelines for out-of-home child care programs* (2nd ed.). Elk Grove Village, IL: American Academy of Pediatrics.

Bardige, B., & Segal, M. (2004). Conversations in child care. *Zero to Three, 25*(1), 16–22.

Brazelton, T. B. (1992). *Touchpoints: Your child's emotional and behavioral development: Birth to 3*. Reading, MA: Addison-Wesley.

Burchinal, M. R., Cryer, D., Clifford, R. M., & Howes, C. (2002). Caregiver training and classroom quality in childcare centers. *Applied Developmental Science, 6*(1), 2–11.

Center for Evidence-Based Practice. (nd). *Recommended practices: Being an evidence-based practitioner.* Retrieved January 24, 2008, from http://challengingbehavior.fmhi.usf.edu/handouts/Practitioner.pdf

Clarke-Stewart, K. A., Vandell, D. L., Burchinal, M., O'Brien, M., & McCartney, K. (2002). Do regulable features of child-care homes affect children's development? *Early Childhood Research Quarterly, 17*(1), 52–86. Also available at www.childcareresearch.org/location/ccrca365

Copa, A., Lucinski, L., Olsen, E., & Wollenburg, K. (1999). Promoting professional and organizational development: A reflective practice model. *Zero to Three, 20*(1), 3–9.

Curtis, D., & Carter, M. (2003). *Designs for living and learning: Transforming early childhood environments.* St. Paul, MN: Redleaf Press.

Day, M., & Parlakian, R. (2004). *How culture shapes social–emotional development: Implications for practice in infant-family programs.* Washington, DC: ZERO TO THREE.

Deiner, P. L., & Qiu, W. (2007). Embedding physical activity and nutrition in early care and education programs. *Zero to Three, 28*(1), 13–18.

Dodge, D., Rudick, S., & Burke, K. (2006). *The Creative Curriculum® for infants, toddlers, and twos* (2nd ed.). Washington, DC: Teaching Strategies. (Also available in Spanish)

Family Support America. (2001). *Guidelines for family support practice* (2nd ed.). Chicago: Family Support America.

Genishi, C. (2002). Young English language learners: Resourceful in the classroom. *Young Children, 57*(4), 66–72.

Gorski, P. (1999). Toilet training guidelines: Day care providers: The role of the day care provider in toilet training. *Pediatrics, 103*(6), 1367–1368. Retrieved January 2, 2008, from http://pediatrics.aappublications.org/cgi/content/full/103/6/S1/1367

Hart, B., & Risley, T. (1995). *Meaningful differences in everyday lives.* Baltimore: Brookes.

Healthy Childcare America. (nd). *Back to sleep, tummy to play.* Retrieved January 2, 2008, from www.healthychildcare.org/pdf/SIDStummytime.pdf

Howes, C., Whitebook, M., & Phillips, D. (1992). Teacher characteristics and effective teaching in child care: Findings from the National Child Care Staffing Study. *Child & Youth Care Forum, 21*(6), 3999–4140.

Lally, R. (2005, December). *Intellectual development and language learning in the first three years.* National Association for the Education of Young Children Annual Conference, Washington, DC.

Lally, J. R., & Mangione, P. (1988–2007). *Program for infant toddler care.* Sacramento: California Department of Education Press

Lally, J. R., Torres, Y. L., & Phelps, P. C. (1993, December). *Caring for infants toddlers in groups: Necessary considerations for emotional, social, and cognitive development.* Presentation at ZERO TO THREE's Eighth Biennial National Training Institute, Washington, DC. (Go to www.zerotothree.org/caring.html)

Marzollo, J., & Pinkney, J. (1997) *Pretend you're a cat.* New York: Puffin.

Modigliani, K., & Moore, E. (2005). *Many right ways: Designing your home child care environment* (handbook and video). St. Paul, MN: Redleaf Press.

National Association for the Education of Young Children. (2006). *NAEYC early childhood program standards.* Washington, DC: Author. Retrieved January 30, 2008, from www.naeyc.org/accreditation/standards/Training Resources and Curriculum

National Research Council. (2001). *Eager to learn: Educating our preschoolers.* In Barbara T. Bowman, Suzanne M. Donovan, & M. Susan Burns (Eds.). Washington, DC: National Academy Press.

National Institute of Child Health and Human Development (NICHD) and Early Child Care Research Network (ECCRN). (1996). Characteristics of infant child care: Factors contributing to positive caregiving. *Early Childhood Research Quarterly, 11*(3), 269–306. Also available at www.childcareresearch.org/location/ccrca589

National Institute of Child Health and Human Development (NICHD) and Early Child Care Research Network (ECCRN). (2000). Characteristics and quality of child care for toddlers and preschoolers. *Applied Developmental Science, 4*(3), 116–135. Also available at www.childcareresearch.org/location/ccrca2460

Parlakian, R., & Seibel, N. (2002). *Building strong foundations: Practical guidance for promoting the social–emotional development of infants and toddlers.* Washington, DC: ZERO TO THREE.

Petitto, L., & Dunbar, K. (in press). New findings from educational neuroscience on bilingual brains,. scientific brains, and the educated mind. In K. Fischer & T. Katzin (Eds.), *Building usable knowledge in mind, brain, and education.*New York: Cambridge University Press.

Phillipsen, L. C., Burchinal, M. R., Howes, C., & Cryer, D. (1997). The prediction of process quality from structural features of child care. *Early Childhood Research Quarterly, 12*(3), 281–303. Also available at www.childcareresearch.org/location/ccrca489

Pope, J., & Seiderman, E. (2000). The childcare connection: A meeting ground for parents and the family support movement. *Special Focus on Childcare. America's Family Support Magazine, Winter 2000–01.*

Porter, T., Rice, R., & Rivera, E. (2006). *Assessing quality in family, friend, and neighbor care: The child care assessment tool for relatives.* New York: The Institute for a Child Care Continuum.

Post, J., & Hohmann, M. (2000) *Tender care and early learning: Supporting infants and toddlers in child care settings.* Ypsilanti, MI: High/Scope Press.

Program for Infant Toddler Care. (2007). *The PITC philosophy.* Retrieved January 1, 2008, from www.pitc.org/pub/pitc_docs/about.html

Program for Infant Toddler Caregivers. (nd). *Acknowledge, ask, and adapt communication process.* Retrieved October 12, 2007, from www.pitc.org/cs/pitclib/download/pitc_res/201/Process%20in%20Communicating.pdf?x-r=pcfile_d

Raikes, H. H., Raikes., H. A., Pan, B. A., Luze, G., Tamis-LeMonda., C. S., Rodriguez., E. T., Brooks-Gunn, J., et al. (2006). Mother–child bookreading in low-income families: Correlates and outcomes during the first three years of life. *Child Development, 77*(4), 924–941.

Segal, M., & Masi, W. (2001). *In time and with love: Caring for the special needs infant and toddler.* New York: Newmarket Press.

Seibel, N., Britt, D., Gillespie, L. G., & Parlakian, R. (2006). *Preventing child abuse and neglect.* Retrieved March 18, 2008, from www.zerotothree.org/site/PageServer?pagename=ter_trng_pcan

Torelli, L., & Durrett, C. (nd). *Landscape for learning: The impact of classroom design on infants and toddlers.* Retrieved October 12, 2007, from www.spacesforchildren.com/impact.html

Vandell, D. L., & Wolfe, B. (2002). *Child care quality: Does it matter and does it need to be improved?* Madison: University of Wisconsin-Madison, Institute for Research on Poverty. Also available at www.childcareresearch.org/location/ccrca2144

Watamura, S. E., Donzella, B., Alwin, J., & Gunnar, M. E. (2003). Morning-to-afternoon increases in cortisol concentrations for infants and toddlers at child care: Age differences and behavioral correlates. *Child Development, 74*(4), 1006–1020.

White, R., & Stoecklin, V. (2003). *The great 35 square foot myth.* Kansas City, MO: White Hutchison Leisure and Learning Group. Retrieved October 12, 2007, from www.whitehutchinson.com/children/articles/35footmyth.shtml

Wittmer, D. S., & Petersen, S. H. (2006). *Infant and toddler development and responsive program planning: A relationship-based approach.* Upper Saddle River, NJ: Merrill-Prentice Hall.

Women's Health.gov. (2005). *Benefits of breastfeeding.* Retrieved March 18, 2008, from www.4woman.gov/breastfeeding/index.cfm?page=227

ZERO TO THREE Center for Program Excellence. (2002). *Introducing reflective supervision into an infant/family program.* Washington, DC: Author. Retrieved April 21, 2008, from www.zerotothree.org/cpe/tip_2002_04.html

CHAPTER 3

Tools for Further Learning

This chapter provides a variety of resources for improving developmentally appropriate practice in infant–toddler care and education programs. The first part provides illustrations of developmentally appropriate practice in situations that are typical in programs. This is followed by a useful chart of developmental milestones from birth to 3 years. Finally, a rich collection of resources is listed for further study and deeper understanding.

Reflections on Responsive, Appropriate Practice

The following section provides everyday examples of responsive, appropriate practice. Each is followed by a short reflection on how these kind, thoughtful responses contribute to the quality of the child's experience.

Interactions Among Adults and Children

A young infant awakens in his crib and starts to cry.

An appropriate response. The baby's primary care teacher calls his name in a soft, soothing voice as she walks over to the crib. She smiles and gives the baby a warm hug, holding and soothing him until he is fully awake. She then tells him "Let's change your diaper," patting his diaper to reinforce the message, and walks to the changing table.

Reflections. The baby is quickly acknowledged. He does not have to wonder if he has been heard. This supports his sense of being important and an effective communicator, which builds his trust in his infant care teacher. The teacher shows him affection through a variety of actions, making the transition to being awake a pleasant one, thus helping him with regulation of his state of alertness. She uses language and gestures to help him anticipate the diaper change, which helps build his sense of predictability in the world.

Care teachers cannot always respond immediately to each of the three or four babies in their care. However, by being available as often as possible, the infant care teacher earns the trust of each child that she will respond as quickly as possible.

A young infant, lying on her tummy trying to roll over but failing, begins to fuss and then cry.

An appropriate response. Her care teacher turns to her, saying in a soothing voice, "Are you tired of being on your tummy?" He gently helps the baby roll onto her back. He looks into her eyes, smiling, then makes an exaggerated surprise face and says, "Look what you can do!"

Reflections. This sensitive infant care teacher is able to support the baby's experience. She is on the verge of rolling over at will, buts gets frustrated when she is unsuccessful. The care teacher puts the baby's experience into words, thus letting her know she can be understood. He supports her effort to roll over and then shows pleasure and encouragement with his facial expression and his words.

By positioning two or more babies together on the floor, the infant care teacher makes himself available to each of them while providing opportunities for social interaction among them.

A young infant, on her tummy, drools on the carpet as she enthusiastically gurgles and practices her repertoire of sounds.

An appropriate response. The teacher lies down in front of the baby and copies her sounds. She responds to each sound, then waits, looking into the baby's eyes with anticipation until she makes the next sound. They have a real dialogue going. Without missing a beat, she slips a diaper cloth under the baby's head to keep the carpet clean.

Reflections. This baby is an active conversation partner. Through this back and forth communication, she is learning that she is interesting and has something to offer in this relationship. She is practicing how to

take turns with this engaged, patient infant care teacher. Her subtle placing of the cloth to keep the environment sanitary does not interrupt the dialogue.

A young infant, being fed his bottle, pats his hand on the bottle and looks at his care teacher's face.

An appropriate response. His infant care teacher smiles, stroking his hand and leg gently. She lets him push the bottle away when he wants a break while holding the bottle within his reach. When he is ready, he reaches for the bottle and pulls it back to his mouth. They resume their peaceful rocking, touching, and looking into each other's eyes.

Reflections. This baby and infant care teacher are sharing a wonderful, quiet, intimate moment. The baby feels unhurried, he is able to listen to his own body's messages of hunger or need to pause. The baby is setting the pace for this interaction. His care teacher is showing him that he is important and worth her time and attention.

A mobile infant is fussy because a new tooth is coming in.

An appropriate response. His infant care teacher rocks him in her arms. She tells him, in a loving tone, "I know your mouth doesn't feel good" and touches his lips to show that she knows what hurts. She puts on a CD of Haitian songs his parents brought in, knowing that singing and dancing are an important part of his home life. She sings the few words she knows in Patois. The baby seems to forget the soreness in his gums as they rock to the music, laughing and singing.

Reflections. The infant care teacher shows the baby that she understands that his mouth is hurting and that she is sensitive to his pain. She uses words and music from his home language, and her own attention and closeness, to provide comfort. The comfort and diversion the care teacher provides help him manage his discomfort and participate in play.

Photo credit: Kelly Rozwadowski

A mobile infant, arriving in her mother's arms, clings and cries when her infant care teacher approaches.

An appropriate response. Her teacher greets the baby and her mother. "Ooooh, Sherri. It's hard to say good-bye to Mommy today." To the mother, she says, "How are you doing? This makes it so hard to leave, doesn't it?" Mother and teacher talk about separation issues. As they talk, they watch for signs the infant is relaxing, and nod to each other—it is time. There are hugs, more tears, but the baby is ready to let her care teacher hold her as she waves bye-bye.

Reflections. Mobile infants are able to hold an image of loved ones in their minds so they may be very unhappy when a parent leaves them, knowing that mom or dad are still out there somewhere. She is still too young to understand that her mother will come back every time she leaves. The infant care teacher understands this normal developmental phase and is able to support both baby and mother through difficult separations.

A mobile infant struggles to push a ball up a wide, low ramp.

An appropriate response. The infant care teacher observes the baby's efforts, smiling at her when she turns to look for him. He uses a few words of encouragement and smiles. She tries for a long time and finally succeeds, shrieking with pride and excitement. Her care teacher claps and says, "All right! You rolled the ball all the way to the top!"

Reflections. This baby has been engaged by an interesting problem that she solves by using her body, mind, and relationship with her infant care teacher. She takes great pleasure in her success that is echoed by the infant care teacher who fully appreciates her accomplishment. Even though the infant care teacher has provided enough distance for the baby to accomplish this feat on her own, they are emotionally attuned.

A mobile infant, watching a friend push a piece of a four-piece puzzle over the surface of the board, grabs at the puzzle.

An appropriate response. His teacher sits beside them, gently removing the baby's hands from the puzzle while reaching for a similar puzzle from the shelf in front of them, saying, "Looks like fun, huh? Here's a puzzle for you." She stays to watch them, smiling at the baby as she picks up a piece of the puzzle.

Reflections. This infant care teacher knows that mobile infants are too young to understand another person's point of view and therefore to take turns. The baby who grabbed the puzzle simply did what babies do—go for what they want. The infant care teacher maintained a calm, friendly tone to the play by making sure the first child got his puzzle back while supplying a similar one to the second child.

Photo credit: Stephen Bobb

Two toddlers, playing with a tea set, offer their teacher some imaginary tea and cookies.

An appropriate response. "Oh thank you," the teacher says, as she sits down at the small table. "I love tea parties. And I am sooo hungry. What kind of cookies are these?" "Chocklit chip," says one toddler. "Prinkle cookies," says the other. "Chocolate chip with sprinkles! That's my favorite kind! Ummm. These are so sweet and crunchy! Can you pour me some tea?" asks the teacher. "Here tea," says a toddler. "Thank you. Oh! This tea is burning hot."

Reflections. The care teacher's enthusiastic acceptance of the invitation to tea demonstrates to the toddlers that their play is interesting and their company is valued. Her verbal expansions on their play make for a rich language experience for the toddlers.

A toddler, joining a group playing with large blocks, pushes down a child who is in her way.

An appropriate response. Her infant care teacher quickly picks up the fallen child to soothe her, and tells the toddler in a firm voice, "Take my hand.

Pushing hurts—see, Alisha fell down—let's help her up and then find some blocks so you can play, too."

Reflections. This toddler care teacher maintains a calm demeanor as she helps both toddlers to manage their feelings. Taking the hand of the child who pushed helps direct the child's attention to the teacher as she firmly sets a limit on the child's behavior. She then engages the "pusher" in comforting the child who was pushed down, providing a moment's lesson in empathy. The infant care teacher then responds empathically to the child who wanted to join the builders and model problem solving by settling her in with blocks as well.

Four toddler friends are eating apples at morning snack. When the three English speakers ask the care teacher for second helpings, the one young dual-language learner, Carlos, sits quietly.

An appropriate response. The teacher, sitting with the small group of toddlers, offers the bowl of apple slices to Carlos and asks, "Would you like more?" then watches and responds to his cues.

Reflections. This toddler care teacher understands that while dual-language learners are mastering early language, they can become confused and embarrassed about their vocabulary. A young child may prefer to remain silent rather than make a mistake. The care teacher is able to continue to support Carlos's home language as well as his acquisition of English. The skilled teacher uses language along with gestures to communicate with dual-language learners.

A 2-year-old always refuses to finger paint, play with play dough, or touch anything "icky."

An appropriate response. The toddler care teacher offers him sensory experiences that keep his hands clean, like kneading dough in a plastic bag, sifting and pouring rice, and feeling and talking about the textures in touch-and-feel books. She chooses a relaxed time to introduce finger painting. First, she asks him to help bring over bowls of water and paper towels so that the children can rinse their hands. As she sets out paints, paper, and craft sticks, she explains that the children can use their fingers or the sticks to draw with this thick paint. As he watches, she places a small dab of paint on her paper and, using one finger, begins to draw a face. "This paint feels cool and wet," she says. "Look, I can use my finger to draw a face." Knowing that the paint will feel less gooey to him if he presses down on it purposefully than if he accidentally gets some on his hands, she asks if he would like to help her finish the eyes. Very carefully, he begins.

Reflections. This toddler care teacher understands that children may experience sensory materials very differently from one another. Children who are very sensitive to textures or to touching anything messy respond to an incremental approach like this teacher took in order to feel safe exploring new materials. Using her observation skills to judge his comfort level, she plans to offer him a variety of touch experiences. As she observes his growing comfort and interest, she very gently introduces him to finger painting, leaving him in control of how he will participate and when he will clean his hands. Approaches like this can help children become less sensitive and more comfortable with sensory stimulation.

Family/Infant Care Teacher Interactions: Morning Separations

A mother starting a new job brings her 3-month-old baby to a child care center for the first time.

An appropriate response. The family has visited the center and knows the director and the baby's primary teacher. She knows the center's policies and procedures (e.g., where to put the diaper bag, the labeled bottles of expressed milk, medicine). She has brought a favorite stuffed animal, a special rattle, and some family pictures. Her baby's teacher greets her, and they talk as they walk through the morning routine of putting things away and writing on the daily record. The care teacher observes that leaving their baby is hard for most parents and encourages the

mother to call, visit. and share concerns openly. She lets her know how important it is for parents to be involved as it helps ensure the best care for the baby.

Reflections. It is often difficult to leave a baby in group care for the first time, no matter how good the family feels about the program and the infant care teacher. The infant care teacher knows it is important to help this mother feel confident about the care her baby will receive and know that the infant care teacher is her partner. This mother is feeling welcomed and valued as she begins her experience with child care.

A Mexican American grandmother who occasionally brings her 8-month-old granddaughter to child care has a difficult time leaving.

An appropriate response. A Mexican American woman is the baby's primary teacher and has spent time getting to know the grandmother. She has learned that the grandmother does not approve of child care for babies and feels guilty that she cannot stay home to take care of her granddaughter herself instead of working. Although the infant care teacher is often busy, she asks her colleague to cover her for 10 minutes so she can focus on the grandmother when she brings her granddaughter. She listens, appreciating how much the grandmother loves her grandbaby, how important she is to the family, and how ambivalent she feels about putting her in the care of someone outside of the extended family.

Reflections. Child care can be a struggle for families whose culture relies on and highly values extended families caring for the children. How can something as precious as a baby be left in the hands of strangers? Will she be held as much as the grandmother holds her? Will she be comforted when she cries? Will she be fed the way she is at home?

In some cultures the relationship between elders and children is a two-way street. Elders teach children to receive and accept help, and elders then feel useful, loved, and needed. This care teacher knows it is imperative that she be culturally sensitive and that she gain the family's trust. She understands that for this child to feel comfortable in a child care setting, it is important that all close family members eventually accept the idea of child care. She knows children learn from trusted adults how to assess a situation, thus building a strong, warm relationship with the grandmother is critical to the child's sense of safety and security in the program.

A father and mother work opposite shifts. The mother brings her 12-month-old to the center very early in the morning. The baby is in pajamas and still sleeping. The mother is rushing to get to work.

An appropriate response. Mother knows that center policies ask parents to have their babies in a clean diaper, fed, and dressed for the day. The care teacher sees that the mother is really stressed and tells her not to worry about the policy today. She adds, "Little ones don't always follow our schedules. I'll keep an eye on her while she sleeps and I'll comfort her as soon as she wakes up. I'll tell her you're at work, but you gave her a big kiss!"

Reflections. The infant care teacher has a caring relationship with the families as well as the infant. She knows that this baby sleeps deeply and her schedule is erratic given the reality of her family's life. Although the teacher may need to reassert this policy if the mother's morning rush becomes problematic, she can be flexible for now.

Family/Infant Care Teacher Interactions: Evening Reunions

A father tries to gather up his mobile infant to go home as the baby clings to the infant care teacher.

An appropriate response. The baby's primary infant care teacher can see that this father is in a hurry and tired at the end of an obviously stressful day. She talks to him in a gentle voice, saying, "Your little girl is still feeling that cold she had, so she's a little clingy. I was just reading my babies this story. Could you read it to her a minute while I bring her things? This is a fussy time for all of us, I guess. I know it is for most

babies." The father relaxes as he holds his baby and reads.

Reflections. This infant care teacher is able to support the relationship between this father and his daughter. Babies are sensitive to the moods of the adults in their lives. By helping this father to relax and enjoy a few moments with his daughter, she has probably set the course for them to have a pleasant evening together. She has also strengthened her relationship with the father by being so respectful and sensitive to both his and his baby's feelings and needs.

A mother comes to pick up her 18-month-old who has bitten another child again.

An appropriate response. The child's primary care teacher has called the mother to ask if she can take some time that evening to talk about how to help her son stop biting. The infant care teacher's gentle voice and explanation of what is happening around the biting reassures the mother that biting is normal for an 18-month-old who cannot express his strong feelings in words. Together, they try to identify situations that trigger biting and discuss ways to intervene before it happens.

Reflections. Biting is one of the most common yet upsetting behaviors of toddlers. The toddler care teacher remains calm and engages the mother as a partner in solving the problem. They share insight into what the toddler is trying to do and together develop a plan for addressing the behavior consistently at home and at child care.

A 28-month-old boy is crying as he arrives because his mother is angry and embarrassed that he has wet himself.

An appropriate response. The boy's primary infant care teacher gets a little notebook where she has been recording his efforts to use the toilet. She has learned that this family feels strongly about self-control and appropriate behavior "in school." Other parents are there, so the teacher gently guides the mother to a

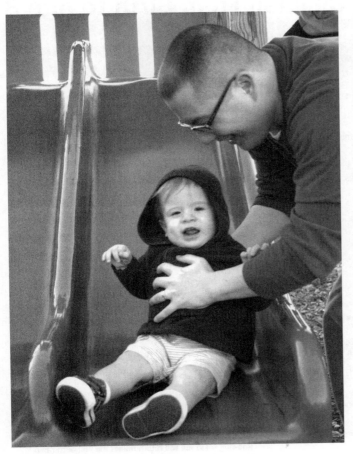

Photo credit: Kelly Rozwadowski

Reflections. The toddler care teacher disagrees with the mother's values about toilet learning, but she knows that supporting the parent–child relationship is her first duty. She is able to demonstrate that the boy is making progress and that there is a calm acceptance of accidents at the program. With the support of the teacher, the mother is able to move from anger to appreciation of her child, leaving the little boy with a positive image of his mother to hold on to during the day.

Out on the playground, a father arrives to see his 30-month-old climbing the ladder to the slide.

An appropriate response. The toddler's primary infant care teacher is watching him as she pushes two toddlers in their T-strap swing seats. She calls to the father, saying that he has arrived just in time to watch a major achievement: the first time up the toddler ladder all by himself. The toddler has fallen before but is determined, and because there is ample shock-absorbent ground cover, she can reassure the father that no one needs to hold him. Father and teacher encourage him with their eyes and applaud his arrival safely at the top. Down he goes into his father's arms.

Reflections. Again, the care teacher is able to support the relationship between parent and child. In a moment that might have been frightening for the parent, or in which he may have tried to hurry his son, the teacher created a situation in which the father could really appreciate and applaud the determination and accomplishment.

sofa, saying softly, "I want to show you something." She opens the book, showing mother and toddler the notes she has on his successes. She asks if the mother can stay to watch him take off his wet pants "all by himself" and help clean himself up. As he does this, she listens to the mother's concerns, knowing that talking will relax her and give her struggling toddler enough time to show her how well he can take off his own pants and wash up. Then they can praise him together.

Developmental Milestones of Children From Birth to Age 3

	I Learn Who I Am	**I Learn About My Feelings**
Birth to 9 Months	**I learn about my body.** I discover that my hands and feet are part of me. I can move them. **I learn to trust your love.** I feel secure when you hold me in your arms. I feel good when you smile at me. **I learn to comfort myself.** I may suck my fingers or hands—it soothes me. **I can make things happen.** I can kick a mobile and make it move. I can smile at you and you will smile back at me.	**I can show you many feelings—pleasure, anger, fear, sadness, excitement, and joy.** I smile and wiggle to show you I like playing with you. I frown or cry when you stop paying attention or playing with me. **Sometimes I need you to help me with my feelings.** I need you to try to understand how I feel. I need you to protect me when I feel overwhelmed or scared. **I share my deepest feelings. I know and trust you.** My smile is brightest for you. I can protest strongly when I am upset. I know you will be there for me no matter what.
From 8 to 18 Months	**How I feel about myself depends on how you care for me and play with me.** I feel competent when you invite me to help you. I feel confident in my abilities when you let me try new things. **I am showing you that my sense of self is growing stronger when I am assertive.** I sometimes insist on doing things my way. When I say, "No!" it often means I am an individual. **I am learning language about me.** I can point to and tell you the names of one or more parts of my body. I begin to use "me," "I," and "mine."	**My feelings can be very strong.** I laugh and may shriek with joy when I am happy and we are having fun. I may sometimes hit, push, or bite because I'm angry or frustrated. **I care deeply about you.** I may smile, hug you, run into your arms, or lean against you to show my affection. I may try to follow you or cling when you get ready to leave. I know now when you're gone, and it frightens me. **Knowing when you will return makes me feel better and helps me learn about time.** I am slowly learning that when those I love leave, they will return. A consistent daily schedule helps me know when things will happen.
From 16 to 36 Months	**Sometimes, I feel powerful. But independence can be scary.** I count on you to set clear and consistent limits that keep me safe. When I test limits, I am learning who I am and how I should behave. **I feel good about myself and where I come from when my culture is reflected in my child care setting.** I feel I belong when you speak to me in my home language. I feel proud when I see pictures of my family and other people like me hanging on the wall. **I sense how you feel about me. Your feelings help shape how I feel about me.** When you respect me, I respect myself. I tune in carefully to your tone and words when you talk about me. **Sometimes I want to be big. Sometimes I want to be a baby again. And sometimes I want to be both—at the same time. This is one of the reasons my behavior is sometimes hard for you to understand. I don't understand it myself.** Sometimes I will walk. Other times I want a ride in the stroller. Sometimes I push you away. Other times I want you to hold me close. It's O.K. — I still love you. **I am learning more self-control.** I understand more often what you expect of me. Sometimes I can stop myself from doing things I shouldn't. Sometimes I can't.	**My feelings can be very strong.** I feel proud of things I make and do. I may be afraid of the dark, monsters, and people in masks or costumes. **I am learning to control my feelings.** I am learning to use words to control my feelings. I sometimes practice how to express my feelings when I play. **I know you have feelings too.** I learn how to care for others by the way you care for me. I sense when you are happy and truly there for me. It makes me feel good.

Note: This list is not intended to be exhaustive. Many of the behaviors indicated here will happen earlier or later for individual infants. The chart suggests an approximate time when a behavior might appear, but it should not be rigidly interpreted.

Often, but not always, the behaviors appear in the order in which they emerge. Particularly for younger infants, the behaviors listed in one domain overlap considerably with several other developmental domains. Some behaviors are placed under more than one category to emphasize this interrelationship.

I Learn About People, Objects, and How Things Work	I Learn to Move and Do	I Learn to Communicate and Relate
I can tell the difference between people I know and people I do not know. I recognize my parents' voices. I relax more when I am with you and other people I know. **I sometimes am afraid of strangers.** I sometimes cry if a stranger gets too close to me or looks at me directly in the eyes. **I like to be with you.** I like to be held by you. I like you to talk softly and smile at me. I smile and "talk" back to you. You are the most important person in my life. **I learn about how the world works.** I like to look around and see new things. I like to play games with you, like peek-a-boo and hide-n-seek.	**At first, my body moves automatically.** I search for something to suck. I turn my head when something blocks my breathing. **Within a few months, I begin to learn to use my fingers and hands.** I put my hand and objects in my mouth. I can move an object from one hand to another. **Over time, I move my body with a purpose.** I can hold my head up. I can roll over. I can crawl by myself. I may even be able to stand up if I hold on to you.	**I can tell you things—even as a newborn.** I cry to tell you I need you. I communicate through the expressions on my face and gestures. **Within a few months, I develop new ways to communicate.** I learn to make many different sounds. I laugh. I use my sounds, change the expression on my face, and move around to get your attention. **I learn to babble.** I make some of the sounds that I hear you use. Sometimes I try to imitate you. I like you to imitate my sounds, too. **I like to "talk" with you—even though I don't yet speak words.** I may catch your eye and smile to tell you I am ready to communicate with you. I stretch my arms toward you when I want you to pick me up.
I am learning about choice and choices. I have favorite toys and favorite foods. I like to choose what to wear. **I like to see and be with other children my age or a little older.** I have fun making silly faces and noises with other children. I do not know yet how to share but I learn through supervised play with others. **I want to be like you.** I learn how to relate to other people by watching how you act with me, our family, and our friends. I feel proud and confident when you let me help you with your "real work," like scrubbing the carrots. **I learn about how the world works.** I am very interested in how the world works. If my music box winds down, I may try to find a way to start it again.	**I am learning to do new things with my fingers and hands.** I can make marks on paper with crayons and markers. I can use a spoon and drink from a cup. **I am learning to move in new ways.** I can sit in a chair. I can pull myself up and stand by holding on to furniture. I learn to walk, first with help and then alone. Sometimes I still like to crawl.	**I communicate through my expressions and actions.** I point to let you know what I want. I may hit, kick, or bite when I get too frustrated or angry. I need you to help me learn how to express these feelings in acceptable ways. **I communicate using sounds and words.** I create long babble sentences. I may be able to say 2 to 10 or more words clearly. **I understand more than you may think—much more than the words I can say.** I listen to you and watch you because I understand more than just words. I learn to look at a ball when you say "ball" in my home language.
I am more aware of other children. I am aware when other children are my age and sex. I am aware of skin color and may begin to be aware of physical differences. **I like to play together with other children.** I may pretend we are going to work or cooking dinner. I build block towers with them. **I am beginning to be aware of other children's rights.** I learn I don't always get my way. Sometimes I can control myself when things don't go my way. Sometimes I can't. **I am becoming aware of how you respond to my actions.** I know when you are pleased about what I do. I know when you are upset with me. **I learn about how the world works.** I may be able to put toys in groups, such as putting all of the toys with wheels together. I can find a familiar toy in a bag, even when I can't see it.	**I can do many new things with my fingers and hands.** I scribble with a crayon or marker and may be able to draw shapes, like circles. I can thread beads with large holes. I am learning to use scissors. **I move in new ways.** I kick and throw a ball. I may be able to walk upstairs putting one foot on each step. **I can handle many everyday routines by myself.** I can dress myself in simple clothes. I can pour milk on my cereal.	**I have many things to tell you.** I learn new words every day, in my home language and sometimes also in a second language. I may know more than 1,000 words by the time I'm 3 years old. I can tell you about things that happened yesterday and about things that will happen tomorrow. **I like you to read and tell me stories.** I especially enjoy stories that are about something I know. Sometimes I may listen for a long time. Other times I may listen for just a little while. Sometimes I like to "read" or tell you a story too. **I play with words.** I like songs, fingerplays, and games with nonsense words. Sometimes I can use an object as if it were something else. For example, I might use a block for a phone.

Resources

Caring: DAP-II is an introduction to early development and the importance of relationships in developmentally appropriate practice. Our understanding of early learning and development is growing rapidly. This chapter provides recommendations for further study.

Development

General Development

Albrecht, K., & Miller, L. (2001). *The infant and toddler child development guide.* Beltsville, MD: Gryphon House.

BFS Entertainment (Producer). (2004). *The baby human* [DVD]. Richmond Hill, Ontario, Canada: Author.

Center on the Developing Child at Harvard University. (2007). *A science-based framework for early childhood policy: Using evidence to improve outcomes in learning, behavior, and health for vulnerable children.* (Available from www.developingchild.harvard.edu)

Gandini, L., & Edwards, C. (Eds.). (2001). *Bambini: The Italian approach to infant and toddler care.* New York: Teachers College Press.

Gonzalez-Mena, J., & Eyer, D. E. (2006). *Infants, toddlers, and caregivers: A curriculum of respectful, responsive care and education* (7th ed.). Boston: McGraw-Hill.

Koralek, D. G., Dombro, A. L., & Dodge, D. T. (2008). *Caring for infants and toddlers* (eCDA ed.). Washington, DC: Teaching Strategies.

Lally, J. R., Mangione, P. L., & Greenwald, D. (2006). *Concepts for care: Essays on infant/toddler development and learning.* San Francisco: WestEd.

Meisels, S. J., Dombro, A. L., Marsden, D. B., Weston, D. R., & Jewkes, A. M. (2003). *The ounce scale.* New York: Pearson Early Learning.

Parlakian, R. (2003). *Before the ABCs: Promoting school readiness in infants and toddlers.* Washington, DC: ZERO TO THREE.

Wittmer, D., & Petersen, S. (2006). *Infant and toddler development and responsive program planning: A relationship-based approach.* Upper Saddle River, NJ: Prentice-Hall.

ZERO TO THREE, Washington, DC. www.zerotothree.org

Brain Development

Eliot, L. (2000). *What's going on in there?: How the brain and mind develop in the first five years of life.* New York: Bantam.

Hawley, T. (2000). *Starting smart: How early experiences affect brain development* (2nd ed.). Washington, DC: ZERO TO THREE.

National Scientific Council on the Developing Child. (2005). *Excessive stress disrupts the architecture of the developing brain. Working Paper No. 3.* Retrieved January 8, 2008, from www.developingchild.net

National Scientific Council on the Developing Child. (2006). *Early exposure to toxic substances damages brain architecture: Working Paper No. 4.* Retrieved January 8, 2008, from www.developingchild.net

Shore, R. (2003). *Rethinking the brain: New insights into early development* (Rev. ed.) New York: Families and Work Institute.

ZERO TO THREE. (2006). *Baby brain map.* Interactive Web site at www.zerotothree.org/site/PageServer?pagename = ter_util_babybrainflash

Cultural Identity Development

Brunson Phillips, C. (1995). Culture: A process that empowers. In J. R. Lally (Ed.), *Infant/toddler caregiving: A guide to culturally sensitive care* (pp. 1–10). Sacramento: California State Department of Education.

Day, M., & Parlakian, R. (2003). *How culture shapes social–emotional development: Implications for practice in infant–family programs.* Washington, DC: ZERO TO THREE.

Derman-Sparks, L. (1995a). Creating an inclusive nonstereotypical environment for infants and toddlers. In P. L. Mangione (Ed.), *Infant/toddler caregiving: A guide to culturally sensitive care* (pp. 64–68). Sacramento: California State Department of Education.

Derman-Sparks, L. (1995b). Developing culturally responsive caregiving practices: Acknowledge, ask and adapt. In P. L. Mangione (Ed.), *Infant/toddler caregiving: A guide to culturally sensitive care* (pp. 40–63). Sacramento: California State Department of Education.

Eggers-Piérola, C. (2005). *Connections and commitments: Reflecting Latino values in early childhood programs.* Portsmouth, NH: Heinemann.

Gonzalez-Mena, J. (2004). *Diversity in early care and education programs: Honoring differences.* Columbus, OH: McGraw-Hill.

Hall, N. S., & Rhomberg, V. (1995). *The Affective Curriculum: Teaching the anti-bias approach to young children.* Toronto, Ontario, Canada: Nelson Canada.

Rogoff, B. (2003). *The cultural nature of human development.* New York: Oxford University Press.

Small, M. F. (1998). *Our babies, ourselves.* New York: Anchor Books.

Trawick-Smith, J. (2006). *Early childhood development: A multicultural perspective.* Upper Saddle River, NJ: Pearson Education.

Zepeda, M., Gonzalez-Mena, J., Rothstein-Fisch, C., & Trumbull, E. (2006). *Bridging cultures in early care and education: A training module.* Mahwah, NJ: Erlbaum.

Emotional Development

Butterfield, P. M., Martin, C. A., & Prairie, A. P. (2004). *Emotional connections: How relationships guide early learning (instructor's manual)* and *Emotional connections: How relationships guide early learning (student text).* Washington, DC: ZERO TO THREE.

Gillespie, L. G., & Seibel, N. L. (2006). Self-regulation: A cornerstone of early childhood development. *Young Children, 61*(4), 34–39.

Honig, A. (2002). *Secure relationships: Nurturing infant/toddler attachment in early care settings.* Washington, DC: National Association for the Education of Young Children.

Lieberman, A. (1994). *The emotional life of the toddler.* New York: The Free Press.

National Scientific Council on the Developing Child. (2004). *Young children develop in an environment of relationships:Working Paper No. 1.* Retrieved January 8, 2008, from www.developingchild.net/reports.shtml

National Scientific Council on the Developing Child. (2004). *Children's emotional development is built into the architecture of their brain: Working Paper No. 2.* Retrieved January 8, 2008, from www.developingchild.net/reports.shtml

Parlakian, R., & Seibel, N. (2002). *Building strong foundations: Practical guidance for promoting the social–emotional development of infants and toddlers.* Washington DC: ZERO TO THREE.

Quann, V., & Wien, C. A. (2006). The visible empathy of infants and toddlers. *Young Children, 61*(4), 22–29.

Siegel, D. J. (1999). *The developing mind: How relationships and the brain interact to shape who we are.* New York: Guilford Press.

Williamson, G. G., & Anzalone, M. E. (2001). *Sensory integration and self-regulation in infants and toddlers: Helping very young children interact with their environment.* Washington, DC: ZERO TO THREE.

Wittmer, D. S. (in press). *Focusing on peers: The importance of relationships in the early years.* Washington, DC: ZERO TO THREE.

Cognitive Development

Astington, J. W., & Barriault, T. (2001). Children's theory of mind: How young children come to understand that people have thoughts and feelings. *Infants and Young Children, 13*(3), 1–12.

Gopnik, A., Meltzoff, A. N., & Kuhl, P. K. (2000). *The scientist in the crib: What early learning tells us about the mind.* New York: Harper Paperbacks.

Lerner, C., & Parlakian, R. (2007). *Learning happens* (DVD with 30 video vignettes). Washington, DC: ZERO TO THREE.

Mangione, P. L., & Lally, J. R. (Eds.). (1990). *Infant/toddler caregiving: A guide to cognitive development and learning.* Sacramento: California State Department of Education.

Language and Literacy Development

Bardige, B., & Segal, M. (2005.). *Building literacy with love: A guide for teachers and caregivers of children from birth through age 5.* Washington, DC: ZERO TO THREE.

Bardige, B., & Segal, M. (2004). Conversations in child care. *Zero to Three, 25*(1), 16–22.

Bardige, B., & Segal, M. (2005). *Poems to learn to read by: Building literacy with love.* Washington, DC: ZERO TO THREE.

Hart, B., & Risley, T. (1995). *Meaningful differences in the everyday experience of young American children.* Baltimore: Brookes.

Lally, J. R., Mangione, P. L., & Young-Holt, C. L. (Eds.). (1990). *Infant/toddler caregiving: A guide to language development and communication.* Sacramento: California State Department of Education.

Pearson, B. Z., & Mangione, P. L. (2006). Nurturing very young children who experience more than one language. In J. R. Lally, P. L. Mangione, & D. Greenwald (Eds.), *Concepts for care* (pp. 31–39). San Francisco: WestEd.

Raines, S., Miller, K., & Curry-Rood, L. (2002). *Story S-t-r-e-t-c-h-e-r-s for infants, toddlers, and twos.* Beltsville, MD: Gryphon House.

Rosenkoetter, S., & Knapp-Philo, J. (Eds.). (2005). *Learning to read the world: Literacy in the first three years.* Washington, DC: ZERO TO THREE.

Sanchez, S. Y. (2005). *Is it wrong to speak to my babies in their home language?: Head Start English language learners toolkit.* Washington, DC: U.S. Department of Health and Human Services.

Stechuk, R. A., Burns, M. S., & Yandian, S. E. (2006). *Bilingual infant/toddler environments: Supporting language and learning in our youngest children: A guide for migrant and seasonal Head Start programs.* Washington, DC: Academy of Educational Development.

Zigler, E., Singer, D. G., & Bishop, S. J. (Eds.). (2004). *Children's play: The roots of reading.* Washington, DC: ZERO TO THREE.

Special Needs

O'Brien, M. (1997). *Inclusive child care for infants and toddlers: Meeting individual needs.* Baltimore, MD: Brookes.

Segal, M., Masi, W. S., & Leiderman, R. (2001). *In time and with love: Caring for infants and toddlers with special needs.* New York: Newmarket Press.

Stephens, K. (2006, Jan/Feb). Creating a coordinated service plan. *Exchange,* 10–17.

Components of Quality

Promotion of Health and Well-Being

American Academy of Pediatrics, American Public Health Association, Health Resources and Services Administration, Maternal and Child Health Bureau. (2002). *Caring for our children: National health and safety performance standards: Guidelines for out-of-home child care programs* (2nd ed.). Elk Grove Village, IL: American Academy of Pediatrics.

Deiner, P. L., & Qiu, W. (2007). Embedding physical activity and nutrition in early care and education programs. *Zero to Three, 28*(1), 13–18.

Gorski, P. (1999). Toilet training guidelines: Day care providers—The role of the day care provider in toilet training. *Pediatrics, 103*(6), 1367–1368. Retrieved January 9, 2008, from http://pediatrics.aappublications.org/cgi/content/full/103/6/S1/1367

Healthy Childcare America. (nd). *Back to sleep, tummy to play.* Retrieved January 9, 2008, from www.healthychildcare.org/pdf/SIDStummytime.pdf

ZERO TO THREE. (2007). Preventing childhood obesity. *Zero to Three, 28*(1).

Developmentally Appropriate Practice

Bredekamp, S., & Copple, C. (Eds.). (1997). *Developmentally appropriate practices in early childhood programs.* Washington, DC: National Association for the Education of Young Children.

Cryer, D., & Harms, T. (Eds.). (2000). *Infants and toddlers in out-of-home care.* Baltimore: Brookes.

Lally, J. R., & Mangione, P. L. (2006). The uniqueness of infancy demands a responsive approach. *Young Children, 61*(4), 14–21.

National Association for the Education of Young Children. (2008). *Draft NAEYC position statement on developmentally appropriate practice, 2008 Revision.* Retrieved March 13, 2008, from www.naeyc.org/about/positions/pdf/draftdap0208.pdf

Curriculum Ideas

Albrecht, K., & Miller, L. (2000a). *Innovations: The comprehensive infant curriculum.* Beltsville, MD: Gryphon House.

Albrecht, K., & Miller, L. (2000b). *Innovations: The comprehensive toddler curriculum.* Beltsville, MD: Gryphon House.

Dodge, D., Rudick, S., & Burke, K. (2006). *The Creative Curriculum® for infants, toddlers, and twos* (2nd ed.). Washington, DC: Teaching Strategies. (Also available in Spanish)

Johnson, J., & Johnson, T. (2006). *Do-it-yourself early learning: Easy and fun activities and toys from everyday home center materials.* St. Paul, MN: Redleaf Press.

Miller, K. (1999). *Simple steps.* Beltsville, MD: Gryphon House.

Miller, K. (2000). *Things to do with toddlers and twos* (Revised ed.). Marshfield, MA: TelShare Publishing.

Miller, K. (2005). *Simple transitions for infants and toddlers.* Beltsville, MD: Gryphon House.

Petersen, S., & Wittmer, D. (2008). *Endless opportunities for infant toddler curriculum: A relationship-based approach.* Upper Saddle River, NJ: Prentice Hall.

Post, J., & Hohmann, M. (2000). *Tender care and early learning: Supporting infants and toddlers in child care settings.* Ypsilanti, MI: High/Scope Press.

Segal, M. (1998a). *Your child at play: Birth to one year: Discovering the senses and learning about the world.* New York: Newmarket Press.

Segal, M. (1998b). *Your child at play: One to two years: Exploring, daily living, learning and making friends.* New York: Newmarket Press.

Segal, M. (1998c). *Your child at play: Two to three years: Growing up, language, and the imagination.* New York: Newmarket Press.

Environments

Curtis, D., & Carter, M. (2003). *Designs for living and learning: Transforming early childhood environments.* St. Paul, MN: Redleaf Press.

Greenman, J. (2005). *Caring spaces, learning places (children's environments that work).* Redmond, WA: Exchange Press.

Isbell, R., & Isbell, C. (2003). *The complete learning spaces book for infants and toddlers: Fifty-four integrated areas with play experiences.* Beltsville, MD: Gryphon House.

Torelli, L. (2002, Spring). Enhancing development through classroom design in Early Head Start. *The Magazine of the National Head Start Association, Children and Families.*

Torelli, L., & Durrett, C. (2001). *Landscape for learning: The impact of classroom design on infants and toddlers.* Retrieved November 11, 2007, from www.spacesforchildren.com/landc1.pdf

Program Structures That Support Relationships

Baker, A. C., & Manfredi/Petitt, L. A. (2004). *Relationships: The heart of quality care: Creating community among adults in early care settings.* Washington, DC: National Association for the Education of Young Children.

Brown-Lyons, M., Robertson, A., & Layzer, J. (2001). *Kith and kin: Informal child care: Highlights from recent research.* Columbia University, Mailman School of Public Health: The National Center for Children in Poverty.

Fenichel, E. (Ed.). (1992). *Learning through supervision and mentorship to support the development of infants, toddlers and their families.* Washington, DC: ZERO TO THREE.

Florida State University Center for Prevention and Early Intervention Policy. (2003). *Ten components of quality child care fact sheet:* Tallahassee, FL. Author. Retrieved November 6, 2007, from www.cpeip.fsu.edu/resourceFiles/resourceFile_1.pdf?CFID = 13219&CFTOKEN = 56126762

Gilkerson, L., & Shamoon-Shanok, R. (2000). Relationships for growth: Cultivating reflective practice in infant, toddler, and preschool programs. In J. D. Osofsky & H. E. Fitzgerald (Eds.), *WAIMH handbook of infant mental health: Vol. 2. Early intervention, evaluation, and assessment* (pp. 34–79). New York: Wiley.

Greenman, J., Stonehouse, A., & Schweikert, G. (2007). *Prime times: A handbook for excellence in infant and toddler care.* St. Paul, MN: Redleaf Press.

Howes, C. (1998). Continuity of care: The importance of infant, toddler, caregiver relationships. *Zero to Three, 18*(6), 7–11.

Leinfelder, J., & Segal, M. (2006). *Coaching for quality: A field guide for directors, consultants, and trainers.* Washington, DC: ZERO TO THREE.

Parlakian, R. (2002). *Reflective supervision in practice: Stories from the field.* Washington, DC: ZERO TO THREE.

Theilheimer, R. (2006). Molding to the children: Primary caregiving and continuity of care. *Zero to Three, 26*(3), 50–54.

Williamson, S. (2006). Challenge or strength? Caring for infants and toddlers in mixed-age groups in family child care. *Young Children, 61*(4), 40–45.

Family and Community Partnerships

Working With Families

Balaban, N. (2006). *Everyday goodbyes: Starting school and early care—A guide to the separation process.* New York: Teachers College Press.

Barrera, I., Corso, R. M., & Macpherson, D. (2003). *Skilled dialogue: Strategies for responding to cultural diversity in early childhood.* Baltimore: Brookes.

Brazelton, T. B., & Sparrow, J. (2006). *Touchpoints: Your child's emotional and behavioral development.* Cambridge, MA: Da Capo Press.

Dombro, A. L., & Lerner, C. (2006). Sharing the care of infants and toddlers. *Young Children, 61*(1), 29–33.

Gowen, J. W., & Nebrig, J. B. (2002). *Enhancing early emotional development. Guiding parents of young children.* Baltimore: Brookes.

Green, S. (2003). Reaching out to fathers: An examination of staff efforts that lead to greater father involvement in early childhood programs. *Early Childhood Research and Practice, 5*(2). Retrieved February 15, 2008, from http://ecrp.uiuc.edu/v5n2/green.html

Lerner, C., & Dombro, A. (2004). *Bringing up baby: Three steps to making good decisions in your child's first years.* Washington, DC: ZERO TO THREE.

Pawl, J., & Dombro, A. (2001). *Learning and growing together with families: Partnering with parents to support young children's development.* Washington, DC: ZERO TO THREE.

Powers, S. (Ed.). (2007). Parental substance abuse. *Zero to Three, 27*(4).

Community Connections

Early Head Start National Resource Center. (2002). *Pathways to prevention: A comprehensive guide for supporting infant and toddler mental health.* Washington, DC: Head Start Information and Publications Center. Retrieved December 3, 2007, from www.headstartinfo.org/pdf/Pathwaysto.pdf

Johnston, K., & Brinamen, C. (2006). *Mental health consultation in child care: Transforming relationships among directors, staff, and families.* Washington, DC: ZERO TO THREE.

Laurion, J., & Schmiedicke, C. (2005). *Creating connections: How to lead family child care support groups.* St. Paul, MN: Redleaf Press.

Pope, J., & Seiderman, E. (2000, Winter). The childcare connection: A meeting ground for parents and the family support movement. *Special Focus on Childcare: America's Family Support Magazine.*

Responsible Financial and Program Management

Carter, M., & Curtis, D. (1998). *The visionary director: A handbook for dreaming, organizing & improvising in your center.* St. Paul, MN: Redleaf Press.

Kreader, J. L., Ferguson, D., & Lawrence, S. (2005, August). Impact of training and education for caregivers of infants and toddlers: Child care and early education research connections. *Research-to-Policy Connections, 3: National Center for Children in Poverty (NCCP).* Retrieved October 8, 2007, from www.childcareresearch.org/discover/pdf/RTPC3.pdf

Parlakian, R. (2001). *Look, listen, and learn: Reflective supervision and relationship-based work.* Washington, DC: ZERO TO THREE.

Pawl, J., & St. John, M. (1995). *How you are is as important as what you do.* Washington, DC: ZERO TO THREE.

Porter, T., Rice, R., & Rivera, E. (2006, April). *Assessing quality in family, friend and neighbor care: The child care assessment tool for relatives, a new paper released by the Institute for a Child Care Continuum at Bank Street College of Education.* New York: Institute for a Child Care Continuum, Bank Street College of Education.

Talan, T. N., & Bloom, P. J. (2004). *Program administration scale: Measuring early childhood leadership and management.* New York: Teacher's College Press.

Whitebook, M., Sakai, L., Gerber, E., & Howes, C. (2001). *Then and now: Changes in child care staffing, 1994–2000, Technical Report.* A joint project of the Center for the Child Care Workforce (CCW) and the Institute of Industrial Relations. Available at www.ccw.org/pubs/Then&Nowfull.pdf

Systems That Support Quality

Making the Case for Investing Early

Heckman, J. J. (2006). Skill formation and the economics of investing in disadvantaged children. *Science 312*(5782), 1900–1902.

Heckman, J., Grunewald, R., & Reynolds, A. (2006). The dollars and cents of investing early: Cost-benefit analysis in early care and education. *Zero to Three, 26*(6), 10–17.

Jadotte, J. P., Golin, S. C., & Gault, B. (2002). *Building a stronger child care workforce: A review of studies of the effectiveness of public compensation initiatives.* Washington, DC: Institute for Women's Policy Research.

National Association of Child Care Resource and Referral Agencies. (2007). *2006 price of child care.* Retrieved May 1, 2007, from www.naccrra.org/randd/data/2006PriceofChildCare.pdf

Peisner-Feinberg, E., Burchinal, M., Clifford, R., Culkin, M., Howes, C., Kagan, S., et al. (1999). *The children of the cost, quality, and outcomes study go to school: Executive Summary.* Chapel Hill: University of North Carolina at Chapel Hill, Frank Porter Graham Child Development Center.

Licensing and Program Standards, Accreditations, Early Learning Guidelines, and Quality Rating Systems

Harms, T., Cryer, D., & Clifford, R. M. (2006). *Infant/Toddler Environment Rating Scale* (Rev. ed.). New York: Teachers College Press.

Harms, T., Cryer, D., & Clifford, R. M. (2007). *Family Child Care Environment Rating Scale.* New York: Teachers College Press.

National Association for Family Child Care. (2005). *Quality standards for NAFCC Accreditation* (4th ed.). Salt Lake City, UT: Author. Retrieved January 8, 2008, from www.nafcc.org/documents/QualStd.pdf

National Association for the Education of Young Children. (2006). *NAEYC early childhood program standards.* Washington, DC: author. Retrieved January 18, 2008, from www.naeyc.org/accreditation/standards/Training Resources and Curriculum

National Child Care Information Center (NCCIC). (2005). *Infant/toddler care and quality rating systems.* Fairfax, VA: Author.

National Child Care Information Center. This Web site provides links to most states licensing and program standards, early learning guidelines, and quality rating systems along with a wide variety of other information (www.NCCIC.org).

Office of Human Development Services, Department of Health and Human Services (2005). Title 45, Chapter XIII, Part 1304—Program Performance Standards for the Operation of Head Start Programs by Grantee and Delegate Agencies.

Petersen, S., Jones, L., & McGinley, K. A. (2008). *Early learning guidelines for infants and toddlers: Recommendations to states.* Washington, DC: ZERO TO THREE.

Schmalzried, B. (2006). *Developmental Learning Activity Standards for NAFCC Accreditation, Environment Standards for NAFCC Accreditation, Health Standards for NAFCC Accreditation, Professional and Business Practice Standards for NAFCC Accreditation, Relationship Standards for NAFCC Accreditation, and Safety Standards for NAFCC Accreditation.* Salt Lake City, UT: National Association for Family Child Care.

Scott-Little, C., Kagan, S. L., & Frelow, V. S. (2007). *Infant–toddler early learning guidelines: Results and implications from analyses of the content addressed.* Greensboro: University of North Carolina.

Policies

Bardige, B. (2005). *At a loss for words: How America is failing our children and what we can do about it.* Philadelphia: Temple University Press.

Brazelton, T. B., & Greenspan, S. I. (2000). *The irreducible needs of children: What every child must have to grow, learn, and flourish.* New York: Perseus.

Cohen, J., Onunaku, N., Clothier, S., & Poppe, J. (2005). *Helping young children succeed: Strategies to promote early childhood social and emotional development. Early Childhood Research and Policy Report.* Washington, DC: National Conference of State Legislatures. Retrieved April 21, 2008, from www.zerotothree.org/site/DocServer/help_yng_child_succeed.pdf?docID = 621

Goldstein, A., Lombardi, J., & Schumacher, R. (2006). Birth to 5 and beyond: A growing movement in early education. *Zero to Three, 26*(6), 41–47.

Hamm, K., Gault, B., & Jones-DeWeever, A. (2005). *In our own backyard: Local and state strategies to improve the quality of family childcare.* Washington, DC: Institute for Women's Policy Research.

Kagan, S. L., & Rigby, E. (2003). Improving the readiness of children for school Brief No. 2. In *State policies that work: A series of policy briefs from the Policy Matters project.* Washington, DC: Center for the Study of Social Policy. Retrieved August 8, 2007, from www.gettingready.org/matriarch/d.asp?PageID = 294&PageName2 = NM503&p = &PageName = Policy + Matters + SR + Brief%2Edoc

Kauerz, K. (2001). *Starting early, starting now: A policymaker's guide to early care and education and school success.* Denver, CO: Education Commission of the States.

Lally, J. R. (1995). The impact of childcare practices and policies on the identity formation of infants and toddlers. *Young Children, 50*(11), 58–67.

Lally, J. R., Luri-Hurvitz, E., & Cohen, J. (2006). Good health, strong families, and positive early learning experiences: Promoting better public policies for America's infants and toddlers. *Zero to Three, 26*(6), 6–9.

Lombardi, J. (2002). *Time to care: Redesigning child care to promote education, support families, and build communities.* Philadelphia: Temple University Press.

Lombardi, J., & Bogle, M. (Eds.). (2004). *Beacon of hope: The promise of Early Head Start for America's youngest children.* Washington, DC: ZERO TO THREE.

Rappaport, D. M., & Yarbrough, K. (2006). Ensuring a bright future for babies: How to advocate effectively for infants and toddlers. *Zero to Three, 26*(6), 20–25.

Schumacher, R., Hamm, K., Goldstein, A., & Lombardi, J. (2006). *Starting off right: Promoting child development from birth in state early care and education initiatives.* Washington, DC: Center for Law and Social Policy.

Zigler, E., Finn-Stevenson, M., & Hall, N. W. (2004). *The first three years and beyond: Brain development and social policy.* New Haven, CT: Yale University Press.

Professional Development

Bredekamp, S., & Willer, B. (1992). Of ladders and lattices, cores and cones: Conceptualizing an early childhood professional development system. *Young Children, 47*(3), 47–50.

Campbell, N. D., Appelbaum, J., Martinson, K., & Martin, E. (2000). *Be all that we can be: Lessons from the military for improving our nation's child care system.* Washington, DC: National Women's Law Center.

McMullen, M. B., & Dixon, S. (2006). Building on common ground: Unifying practice with infant/toddler specialists through a mindful, relationship-based approach. *Young Children, 61*(4), 46–51.

National Child Care Information Center (NCCIC). (2007). *Demand, supply, and quality: Trends in infant/toddler child care in the United States.* Retrieved May 2, 2007, from http://nccic.org/pubs/qcare-it/demand.html

National Research Council. (2001). *Eager to learn: Educating our preschoolers.* Committee on Early Childhood Pedagogy. B. T. Bowman, S. M. Donovan, & M. S. Burns (Eds.), Commission on Behavioral Sciences and Education. Washington, DC: National Academy Press.

Stahl, D., Sazer O'Donnell, N., Sprague, P., & López, M. (2003). *Sparking connections: Community-based strategies for helping family, friend and neighbor caregivers meet the needs of employees, their children and employers.* New York: Families and Work Institute/Washington, DC: Center for Law and Social Policy.

Research of National Importance

Galinsky, E. (2006). *The economic benefits of high-quality early childhood programs: What makes the difference?* Washington, DC: Committee on Economic Development. Retrieved August 12, 2007, from www.ced.org/docs/report/report_prek_galinsky.pdf

National Research Council & Institute of Medicine. (2000). *From neurons to neighborhoods: The science of early childhood development.* Committee on Integrating the Science of Early Childhood Development. Jack. P. Shonkoff & Deborah. A. Phillips (Eds.). Board on Children, Youth, and Families, Commission on Behavioral and Social Sciences and Education. Washington, DC: National Academy Press.

National Institute of Child Health and Development (NICHD) Early Child Care Research Network. (1993–2008). *The NICHD study of early care and youth development: Publications and presentations.* Retrieved February 19, 2008, from http://secc.rti.org/publications.cfm

Office of Planning, Research, and Evaluation. (1996–2008). *Early Head Start research and evaluation project: Reports.* Retrieved February 18, 2008, from www.acf.hhs.gov/programs/opre/ehs/ehs_resrch/index.html

Additional Video/DVDs

Derman-Sparks, L. & The ABC Task Force. (1989). *Anti-bias curriculum: Tools for empowering young children: Curriculum guide.* Washington, DC: National Association for the Education of Young Children.

Begin with love. (2000). Videocassette. Civitas Production. Available from the National Association for the Education of Young Children.

Can I play too? (1994). Produced by Partnerships for Inclusion, Frank Porter Graham Center, Suite 300, Nation's Bank Plaza, 137 Franklin Street, Chapel Hill, NC 27514.

Caring for infants and toddlers: A video series. Produced by Chip Donahue, University of Wisconsin—Extension. Distributed by AIT, Box A, Bloomington, IN 47402-0120.

Living, loving, and learning: Providing quality care for infants and toddlers. (1993). Lincoln, NE: NETCHE

Getting to know you: Developing relationships with infants and toddlers. (1993). Lincoln, NE: NETCHE

Follow the leader: Individualizing care for infants and toddlers. (1993). Lincoln, NE: NETCHE

Health, safety, and nutrition: Building blocks of quality care for infants and toddlers. (1993). Lincoln, NE: NETCHE

Empowering places and spaces: Preparing environments for infants and toddlers. Child care and the ADA. (1993). Produced by Eastern Washington University, Center for Technology in Education and the Community, Paulson Building, Suite 421, West 407 Riverside Road, Spokane, WA 99201.

Communication and learning: The child care collection at Ball State University. (2003). (Available from NAEYC in VHS and DVD)

Cooing, crying, and cuddling: Infant brain development (video and guide). (1998). Muncie, IN: Ball State University.

Laughing, learning, loving: Toddler brain development (video and guide). (1998). Muncie, IN: Ball State University.

Infant curriculum: Great explorations. (2004). Videocassette. South Carolina Educational Television Production. Available from National Association for the Education of Young Children.

Language is the key. Two 20-minute videos, plus a resource guide. Seattle, WA: Washington Learning Systems available at www.walearning.com/languagekey.html. (Available in English, Spanish, Korean, Vietnamese, Mandarin, and Filipino)

Talking and books and *Talking and play.* Seattle, WA: Washington Learning Systems.

Let babies be babies: Caring for infants and toddlers with love and respect: A video series. Distributed by The Family Day Care Association of Manitoba, 203-942 Street Mary's Road, Winnipeg, Manitoba, Canada R2M 3R5.

Available from Child Development Media, *Let babies be babies series,* www.childdevelopmentmedia.com
   Rethinking infants and toddlers
   Keeping babies healthy and safe
   Helping babies learn
   Guiding the journey to independence
   Understanding the partnership with parents
   Caring for the caregiver

My kind of place: Identifying quality infant/toddler care. Produced by the Quality Care for Infants and Toddlers Project of Greater Minneapolis Day Care Association. Distributed by Greater Minneapolis Day Care Association, 1628 Elliot Avenue South, Minneapolis, MN 55404.

New perspectives on infant/toddler learning, development, and care. (2006). Set of three DVDs. Produced by J. R. Lally for the California Department of Education. Sacramento, CA: CDE Press.

Pope, J., & Seiderman, E. (2000, Winter). The childcare connection: A meeting ground for parents and the family support movement. *Special Focus on Childcare: America's Family Support Magazine.*

The program for infant/toddler caregivers: Video series, J. Ronald Lally, Executive Producer. California Department of Education, P.O. Box 944271, Sacramento, CA 95812-0271. (Available in English, Spanish, and Cantonese)

   1995. *Protective urges: Working with the feelings of parents and caregivers*
   1992. *Essential connections: 10 keys to culturally sensitive child care*
   1991. *Discoveries in infancy: Cognitive development and learning*
   1991. *Together in care: Meeting the intimacy needs of infants and toddlers in groups*
   1990. *Getting in tune: Creating nurturing relationships with infants and toddlers.*
   1990. *Flexible, fearful or feisty: The different temperaments of infants and toddlers*
   1989. *It's not just routine: Diapering, feeding and napping infants and toddlers*
   1989. *The three ages of infancy: Caring for young, mobile and older infants*
   1988. *First moves: Welcoming a child to a new caregiving setting.*
   1988. *Space to grow: Creating a child care environment for infants and toddlers*
   1987. *Respectfully yours: Magda Gerber's approach to professional infant/toddler care*

Seeing infants with new eyes. (1984). Videocassette. South Carolina Educational Television. Available from the National Association for the Education of Young Children.

Ten things every child needs. (1997). Chicago, IL: McCormick Tribune Foundation. (www.rrmtf.org/education/10video.htm)

Web Sites

Center for the Childcare Workforce Web site has policy and initiative information, resources and publications to support professionals who care for and educate young children (www.ccw.org).

Center on the Social and Emotional Foundations of Early Learning has complete teaching modules on supporting emotional development and managing challenging behaviors in young children (www.csefel.uiuc.edu).

Child Care and Early Education Research Connections is a comprehensive online collection of research and resources for child care and early education (www.childcareresearch.org).

Early Childhood Learning and Knowledge Center (ECLKC) is offered by the Administration of Children and Families, Office of Head Start. ECKLC has a variety of articles, resources, and online lessons (http://eclkc.ohs.acf.hhs.gov/hslc).

Early Head Start National Resource Center has publications, audioconferences, and webcasts online (www.ehsnrc.org).

National Association for the Education of Young Children is a leading professional association for early childhood. The Web site provides accreditation information, articles, position papers, and events (www.NAEYC.org).

National Association for Family Child Care provides information on accreditation and information to "promote quality care by strengthening the profession of family child care" (www.nafcc.org).

National Center for Children in Poverty provides articles, data, and resources for children at risk because of poverty (www.nccp.org).

National Child Care Information Center is a clearinghouse for articles, data, and information on every aspect of child care (www.nccic.org).

National Dissemination Center for Children With Disabilities provides excellent state resources and contacts on disabilities and disability-related issues pertaining to children and youth (birth to age 22 years) (www.nichcy.org).

National Early Childhood Technical Assistance Center provides information on the Individuals With Disabilities Education Act including articles, contacts, and data on the program for infants and toddlers (www.nectac.org).

National Head Start Family Literacy Center provides resources on family literacy as part of early childhood programs (www.sonoma.edu/cihs/familyliteracy).

National Infant and Toddler Child Care Initiative at ZERO TO THREE has information on initiatives, data, and articles on infant toddler care (www.nccic.org/ITCC).

ZERO TO THREE: The National Center for Infants, Toddlers, and Families provides a wealth of information on health, development, programs, and local, state, and national policies, as well as publications. Links lead to training opportunities, the *Zero To Three* Journal, the Policy Center, the Early Head Start National Resource Center @ ZERO TO THREE, and the National Infant Toddler Child Care Initiative (www.zerotothree.org).